D1062767

FUNERAL SERVICES

FUNERAL SERVICES

BY JAMES L. CHRISTENSEN

FLEMING H. REVELL COMPANY

Except where marked otherwise, the Scripture quotations in this book are from the *Revised Standard Version of the Bible,* copyrighted 1946 and 1952 by the Division of Christian Education, National Council of Churches, and used by permission.

Acknowledgment is made to the following for permission to reprint copyrighted and other material from the sources indicated:

THE BETHANY PRESS for material from *Christian Worship: A Service Book,* ed. by G. Edwin Osborn, copyright, 1953 by Wilbur H. Cramblet.

THE BOBBS-MERRILL COMPANY, INC., for "Away" from *Afterwhiles* by James Whitcomb Riley.

CHAPPELL AND COMPANY, INC., for "There Is No Death," copyright by Chappell and Company, Inc. Used by permission.

DOUBLEDAY & CO., INC., for material from Introduction by Will Rogers in *Trails Plowed Under* by Charles Russell. Copyright, 1927, by Doubleday & Co. Reprinted by permission of the publisher.

CARL FISCHER, INC., for "Open the Gates of the Temple" by Mrs. Joseph F. Knapp.

HARPER & BROTHERS for material, identified in Notes at the end of this book, from *The Funeral Encyclopedia,* ed. by Charles L. Wallis and reprinted by permission of Harper & Brothers; for "An Epitaph" by Edwin Markham from *Poems of Edwin Markham,* ed. by Charles L. Wallis, and reprinted by permission of Harper & Brothers.

HOPE PUBLISHING COMPANY for "Leave It There" by C. Albert Tindley.

NATIONAL SELECTED MORTICIANS for "How Beautiful To Be with God" from *Wayside Altar,* and quotation from the Rev. Robert J. Burdette, both in *A Service Book* ed. by W. Halsey Smith.

New Century Leader, a David C. Cook publication, for quotation by Bishop Berggrav of Norway in December, 1956, issue.

New York *Herald Tribune* and *The Reader's Digest* for "I Die at Dawn," copyright, 1942, by The Reader's Digest Association, Inc.

HOUGHTON, MIFFLIN CO. and the Estate of Francis G. Peabody for prayer, "For a Young Person," from *Prayers for Various Occasions and Needs.*

REILLY & LEE CO. for "When Sorrow Comes" from *When Day Is Done* by Edgar A. Guest.

G. SCHIRMER, INC. for "I Walked Today Where Jesus Walked" by Daniel S. Twohig and Geoffrey O'Hara.

To

Charles E. Hannan

whose influence led me to the Christian ministry

and whose Pastor's heart is my inspiration and example

To

Charles B. Hooton

whose influence I d we to the Christian ministry

and whose Pastor's heart is my inspiration and example

Contents

CONTENTS

8

FUNERAL SERVICES

I

For an Infant

(*To be used at graveside or in chapel*)

Scripture Reading:

"The Lord is my shepherd, I shall not want; he makes
me lie down in green pastures. He leads me beside still
waters. . . . Even though I walk through the valley of
the shadow of death, I fear no evil; for thou art with
me . . ." (Psalm 23:1, 2, 4).

"He will feed his flock like a shepherd, he will gather the
lambs in his arms, he will carry them in his bosom . . ."
(Isaiah 40:11).

Prayer:

O God, whose Son took little children in His arms and
blessed them, enable us, we beseech Thee, to entrust the
soul of this child to Thy never-failing care and love, and
bring us all to Thy heavenly abode, through the same Son,
Jesus Christ, our Lord. Amen.

Meditation:

INTO GOD'S HEAVENLY GARDEN

In the most beautiful gardens, though carefully tended
by the most skillful botanist, there is an occasional rose
that buds, but never opens. In all respects the rose is like
all the others but some unseen cause keeps it from blooming.

It wilts and fades away without coming to its radiant unfolding.

What happens in nature's garden occasionally happens also in the garden of God's human family. A baby is born, beautiful, precious—but with some unseen, mysterious band sealing that life so that it can never come to its rightful unfolding. This child, too, like the bud that never fully opens, gradually fades away to be gathered back into God's heavenly garden of souls where all imperfections are made perfect; all injustices are made right; all mysteries are explained; and all sorrows turned to happiness.

Into the skilled hands of God we must entrust the care of this infant, just as Mrs. M. E. Smith did when she wrote: "An angel came and hushed my baby's cries, and while I prayed that he might stay, stopped his breathing, stiffened his little limbs, and bore his spirit to heaven. On the brow was written with God's own finger, Everlasting peace; on the still breast, Perfect purity; in the palms of the little hands, No rough scars of earthly work shall ever stain them; on the white round feet, Earth's thorns shall never wound them; on the sealed eyelids, No tears shall wet them; and on the serene lips, No cry of pain shall pass them.[1]

Confident of the blissful abode of the innocent, we commit this infant into God's heavenly garden of souls.

> Now like a dewdrop shrined
>   Within a crystal stone,
> Thou'rt safe in heaven, my dove!
> Safe with the Source of love,
>   The everlasting One.
> And when the hour arrives
>   From flesh that sets me free
> Thy spirit may await,
>   The first at heaven's gate,
>   To meet and welcome me.[2]

Benediction:

The peace of God, which passeth all understanding, keep your hearts and minds in the knowledge and love of God, and of His Son Jesus Christ our Lord. And the blessing of God Almighty, the Father, the Son, and the Holy Spirit, be amongst you, and remain with you always. Amen.

II

For a Small Child

Organ Prelude:

"O God, Our Help in Ages Past"
"The King of Love My Shepherd Is"
"Lead, Kindly Light"

Opening Scriptural Sentence:

"The eternal God is your dwelling place, and underneath are the everlasting arms" (Deuteronomy 33:27).

"To thee, O Lord, I lift up my soul . . . Turn thou to me, and be gracious to me; for I am lonely and afflicted. Relieve the troubles of my heart, and bring me out of my distresses. Consider my affliction and my trouble, and forgive all my sins" (Psalm 25:1, 16–18).

Hymn: (Optional) "Saviour, Like a Shepherd Lead Us"

(This may be organ music, choral anthem, vocal solo, or spoken)

Saviour, like a shepherd lead us,
　　Much we need Thy tender care;
In Thy pleasant pastures feed us,
　　For our use Thy folds prepare:
Blessed Jesus, Blessed Jesus!
　　Thou has bought us, Thine we are,
Blessed Jesus, Blessed Jesus!
　　Thou hast bought us, Thine we are.

Thou hast promised to receive us,
　　Poor and sinful tho' we be;
Thou hast mercy to relieve us,
　　Grace to cleanse, and power to free:
Blessed Jesus, Blessed Jesus!
　　Early let us turn to Thee,
Blessed Jesus, Blessed Jesus!
　　Early let us turn to Thee.

Early let us seek Thy favor,
　　Early let us do Thy will;
Blessed Lord and only Saviour,
　　With Thy love our bosoms fill:
Blessed Jesus, Blessed Jesus!
　　Thou hast loved us, love us still,
Blessed Jesus, Blessed Jesus!
　　Thou hast loved us, love us still.[1]

(Other appropriate selections: "Brightly Gleams Our
Banner," "He Shall Feed His Flock," "O Love That Wilt
Not Let Me Go," "Angel Voices, Ever Singing.")

Scripture Reading:

"At that time the disciples came to Jesus, saying, 'Who
is the greatest in the kingdom of heaven?' And calling to
him a child, he put him in the midst of them, and said,
'Truly, I say to you, unless you turn and become like children, you will never enter the kingdom of heaven' " (Matthew 18:1–3).

". . . for to such belongs the kingdom of heaven" (Matthew 19:14).

"Thus says the Lord: 'A voice is heard in Ramah, lamentation and bitter weeping. Rachel is weeping for her children; she refuses to be comforted for her children, because they are not.' Thus says the Lord: 'Keep your voice from weeping, and your eyes from tears; for your work shall be rewarded, says the Lord . . .'" (Jeremiah 31:15–16).

"And the streets of the city shall be full of boys and girls playing in its streets" (Zechariah 8:5).

"They shall hunger no more, neither thirst any more; the sun shall not strike them, nor any scorching heat. For the Lamb in the midst of the throne will be their shepherd, and he will guide them to springs of living water; and God will wipe away every tear from their eyes" (Revelation 7:16–17).

Prayer:

O God of love and mercy, we thank Thee that Thou art able to comfort these parents whose joy has been turned into sorrow, whose house has been left desolate by the passing of this little one. We thank Thee for the assurance that their loved one is at rest in Thee and that love can never lose its own. Let the things unseen and eternal grow more real, more present, more full of meaning and power. Let Thy strength sustain their weakness. Free them from any bitterness and fill them with Thy peace, through Jesus Christ our Lord. Amen.

Meditation:

STARGAZING IN THE NIGHT

A little girl was impressed by the stars. She had many questions to ask concerning them. "Are the stars there all the time? Why can't you see them during the day?" Her mother replied, "You can see them only at night. Darkness is always more beautiful if we will look up at the stars rather than into the corners of blackness."[2]

That is what I want us to do today—to go stargazing. We sit in the shadow of a black night of sorrow and grief; and yet we sit in the light of the greatest hope the world has ever known. There are some thoughts that shine out like stars in the midnight sky. If we will fasten our minds upon them, instead of upon the darkness, they will give us comfort.

I

One cluster of stars is this: *We can be thankful rather than resentful.*

Hannah, the mother of the child Samuel, said, "For this child I prayed, and the Lord hath given me my petition which I asked of him." This child also has been the gracious gift and has brought much joy to your life. We can pause in gratitude for the years of happiness that *he* has brought to parents, grandparents, relatives and friends.

We can be thankful too that God is able to salvage some value even out of such tragic happenings. The Scripture declares: "A little child shall lead them," and certainly this event brings the eternal value of life closer to us who are left. Rufus Jones once declared that his boy who died had been a greater influence over him than all the others.

Often the first reaction in bereavement is resentment. Some cry, "Oh, why did God do this to us? Why did God take our baby?" If we more fully understood God, His character, His ways, His purposes, we would see that not everything that happens in this world is God's doing. In fact, this world is filled with happenings that are not God's will at all. Says the Bible, "It is not the will of your Father, that one of these little ones should perish." There are evil forces and even human elements interacting upon all that happens in this world. Therefore, do not be resentful toward God because of the death of this child, rather be thankful for the privilege of *his* life and the precious memories you still have. That is a cluster of stars in the night.

II

Here is another: *Do not think too greatly of your own loss, but think of the joys of children in heaven.*

So much of our grief is self-centered. Our tears are tears of self-pity. If we will think of the glorious place to which the child has gone, it will console us. A mother of a young lad who had died wrote a friend, "I hardly know how to tell you, and I have not told you before simply because I did not have the heart to do so—that our dear boy entered his new life last month. Only the thought of his rich and wonderful experiences in these first days of his new life consoles us, or in any way makes up for the loss we feel in his absence."[3]

A similar incident is recorded in the Old Testament. The Shunammite woman had lost her child. Elisha, the prophet, sent his servant to inquire, "Is it well with thee? Is it well with thy child?" Though the child was dead, she responded, "It is well."

Yes, it is well, for God has provided a house of many mansions, a place for growing boys and girls to play. "The streets of the city shall be filled with boys and girls playing in its streets. . . ." There your child will escape war and find everlasting peace. There no rough work will scar *his* palms; no sin shall darken *his* life. No cry of pain shall ever touch *his* lips. Look at these stars in the darkness and say:

He is not dead—the child of our affection—
　　But gone unto that school
Where he no longer needs our poor protection,
　　And Christ Himself doth rule.

In that great cloister's stillness and seclusion,
　　By guardian angels led,
Safe from temptation, safe from sin's pollution,
　　He lives, whom we call dead.

Day after day we think what he is doing
　　In those bright realms of air;
Year after year, his tender steps pursuing,
　　Behold him grown more fair.

Thus do we walk with him, and keep unbroken
　　The bond which nature gives,
Thinking that our remembrance, though unspoken
　　May reach him where he lives.[4]

Benediction:

"May the God of hope fill you with all joy and peace in believing, so that by the power of the Holy Spirit you may abound in hope. Amen" (Romans 15:13).

Postlude:

"How Firm a Foundation, Ye Saints of the Lord"
"Now Let Every Tongue Adore Thee" (J. S. Bach)

III

For a Boy

Prelude:

"Consolation" (Mendelssohn)
Aria from "The Lord Is Mindful of His Own"

Opening Scriptural Sentence:

"The eternal God is your dwelling place, and underneath
are the everlasting arms . . ." (Deuteronomy 33:27).

"Whoever humbles himself like this child, he is the greatest in the kingdom of heaven. . . . Truly, I say to you, unless you turn and become like children, you will never enter
the kingdom of heaven" (Matthew 18:4, 3).

Invocation:

O merciful Father who dost grant children entrance into
Thy kingdom: Grant us steadfastly to believe that this Thy
child has been taken into the safe keeping of Thine eternal
love, and help us to conform to his innocency and simple
faith, that at length, united with him, we may stand in Thy
presence in fulness of joy; through Jesus Christ, our Lord.
Amen.

Solo: "Open the Gates of the Temple"
(This may be choral anthem)

> Open the gates of the temple,
>   Strew palms on the Conqueror's way;
> Open your hearts, O ye people,
>   That Jesus may enter today.

Hark, from the sick and the dying,
    Forgetting their couches of pain,
Voices, glad voices with rapture,
    Are swelling a glad refrain.

Refrain:
"I know that my Redeemer liveth."
    Canst thou, my heart, lift up thy voice and sing,
"I know that my Redeemer liveth,
    And because He lives, I too, shall live."

Open the gates of the temple,
    Our grand hallelujah be heard;
Open your hearts to the Saviour,
    Make room for the crucified Lord.
Tears and the anguish of midnight
    Are lost in the splendor of day.
They who in sorrow once doubted,
    Are swelling a glad refrain.[1]

Scripture Reading:

(Congregation in unison)—"The Lord is my shepherd, I shall not want; he maketh me lie down in green pastures. He leads me beside still waters; he restores my soul. He leads me in paths of righteousness for his name's sake. Even though I walk through the valley of the shadow of death, I fear no evil; for thou art with me; thy rod and thy staff, they comfort me. Thou preparest a table before me in the presence of my enemies; thou anointest my head with oil, my cup overflows. Surely goodness and mercy shall follow me all the days of my life; and I shall dwell in the house of the Lord for ever" (Psalm 23).

"I lift up my eyes to the hills. From whence does my help come? My help comes from the Lord, who made heaven and earth. He will not let your foot be moved, he who keeps you will not slumber. Behold, he who keeps Israel will neither slumber nor sleep. The Lord is your keeper; the Lord is your shade on your right hand. The sun shall not smite you by day, nor the moon by night. The Lord will keep you from all evil; he will keep your life. The Lord will keep your going out and your coming in from this time forth and for ever-more" (Psalm 121).

"Whoever humbles himself like this child, he is the great-est in the kingdom of heaven. . . . Truly, I say to you, unless you turn and become like children, you will never enter the kingdom of heaven" (Matthew 18:4, 3).

Prayer:

"Almighty God, our Heavenly Father, Thou who hast strengthened Thy children with Thy light and power in all ages, hear us now as we beseech Thee to give us faith in Thy love that will not let us go.

Enable us to wait upon Thee in our time of tribulation. We pray with our Saviour that Thy will be done in our lives. Grant unto us the privilege of hearing Thy will, the vision to perceive it, and the courage to fulfill it.

Thy tender mercies remind us that we are not alone in our sorrow and loss. As we have suffered, so Thou hast suf-fered in giving of Thine only begotten Son. As we have loved, so Thou hast loved more and loved first. If there is pain and death in our lives, so there has been a cross and a crown of thorns in Thine. O God, Thou art ever near when we are afflicted, for Thou hast suffered with us.

In our moment of grief, guide our steps that we may place our trust in Thee. Into Thy hands we commit our lives. And having abided in faith, in hope, and in love, may we see the radiance of a new day. In the name of Him who leads the way out of darkness into light, who conquered the cross with the resurrection, in the name of Christ, we turn to Thee. Amen."[2]

Meditation:

OF SUCH IS THE KINGDOM

My darling boy, so early snatched away
From arms still seeking thee in empty air,
That thou shouldst come to me I do not pray,
Lest, by thy coming, heaven should be less fair.

Stay, rather, in perennial flower of youth,
Such as the Master, looking on, must love;
And send to me the spirit of the truth,
To teach me of the wisdom from above.

Beckon to guide my thoughts, as stumblingly
They seek the kingdom of the undefiled;
And meet me at its gateway with thy key,
The unstained spirit of a little child.[3]

In the First Epistle of John (3:14) we read these precious words, "We know that we have passed out of death into life. . . ." Jesus taught His followers that life was eternal and that death is not the end. Death is only a door through which we pass. Death is only the ship that takes us to an unknown port.

"Two strangers, a small boy and an older man, were fishing from the banks of the Mississippi River. Though the fishing was poor, by the time the sun began to set they had talked of many things. Just at dusk a large river boat was seen moving slowly in the distance. When the boy saw the boat he began to shout and wave his arms, that he might attract the attention of those on the boat. The man watched for some time and then said, 'Son, you are foolish if you think that boat is going to stop for you. It's on its way to some unknown place and it surely won't stop for a small boy.' But suddenly the boat began to slow down and it moved toward the river bank. To the man's amazement, the boat came near enough to the shore that a gangplank was lowered and the boy entered the boat and turned to his new friend and said, 'I am not foolish, Mister. You see, my father is captain of this boat and we are going to a new home up the river.' "⁴

Life is like that. There are times when the ship of death makes an unscheduled stop along the river of life and to our surprise picks up a passenger. Of only one thing we can be confident: Our Father is captain of the boat and it is headed for a new home. Death is not the end of life; it is the beginning of a new adventure upon the river of life.

A young sailor boy was headed overseas. His mother, father, and sweetheart had come to the dock to bid him farewell. It was evident that he was reluctant to go, and his loved ones did not want him to leave. Nonetheless, his time had come. Their eyes filled with tears as they kissed the last time. No one can view a scene like that without the mingled pain of parting and the thrill of new adventure.

In the New Testament we read about the elders of Ephesus who came to the seaport of Miletus to see Paul off on his journey. There on the seashore they counseled and prayed and wept together, and then we are told, "They accompanied him unto the ship." How like death—recapture the scene:

The traveler climbs on board the ship—the loved ones must stop there. As the ship moves out to sea, they bid farewell and wave goodbye. The loved ones watch the ship as it slowly moves out to the horizon. The ship becomes smaller and smaller until it seems only a white cloud just where the sea and sky come down together. Then, as the ship disappears, someone says, "There, she's gone." Gone? Gone where? Just gone from sight—that's all. The ship is the same as before. And at the moment someone on this side says, "There, she's gone,"—there are eyes on the land beyond the sunset watching her and ready to shout, "There she comes."

BEYOND THE HORIZON

When men go down to the sea in ships,
  'Tis not to the sea they go;
Some isle or pole the mariner's goal.
And thither they sail through calm and gale,
  When down to the sea they go.

When souls go down to the sea by ship,
  And the dark ship's name is Death,
Why mourn and wail at the vanishing sail?
Though outward bound, God's world is round,
  And only a ship is Death.

When I go down to the sea by ship,
  And Death unfurls her sail,
Weep not for me, for there will be
A living host on another coast
  To beckon and cry "All Hail."[5]

Hymn: (Optional) "Jesus, Saviour, Pilot Me"

Jesus, Saviour, pilot me.
  Over life's tempestuous sea;
Unknown waves before me roll,
  Hiding rock and treach'rous shoal;
Chart and compass come from Thee:
  Jesus, Saviour, pilot me.

As a mother stills her child,
   Thou canst hush the ocean wild;
Boist'rous waves, obey Thy will
   When Thou say'st to them "Be still."
Wondrous Sovereign of the sea,
   Jesus, Saviour, pilot me.

When at last I near the shore,
   And the fearful breakers roar
'Twixt me and the peaceful rest,
   Then, while leaning on Thy breast,
May I hear Thee say to me,
   "Fear not, I will pilot thee."[6]

Benediction:

"The Lord bless you and keep you: The Lord make his face to shine upon you, and be gracious to you: The Lord lift up his countenance upon you, and give you peace" (Numbers 6:24–26).

Postlude:

"Hark, Hark, My Soul! Angelic Songs Are Swelling"
"Jesus, Saviour, Pilot Me"
"God Be with You"

IV

For a Young Girl

Prelude:

"I Need Thee Every Hour"
"Safe in the Arms of Jesus"

Opening Scriptural Sentence:

"Jesus said to her, 'I am the resurrection and the life; he who believes in me, though he die, yet shall he live, and whoever lives and believes in me shall never die . . .' " (John 11:25–26).

Invocation:

O Lord Jesus Christ, who Thyself didst weep beside the grave, and art touched with the feeling of our sorrows, fulfill now Thy promise that Thou wilt not leave Thy people comfortless, but wilt come to them. Reveal Thyself unto Thine afflicted servants, and cause them to hear Thee saying, "I am the resurrection and the life." Help them, O Lord to turn to Thee with true discernment and to abide in Thee through living faith; that, finding now the comfort of Thy presence, they may have also a sure confidence in Thee for all that is to come; until the day break, and these shadows flee away. Hear us for Thy great mercy's sake, O Jesus Christ, our Lord. Amen.

Solo: (Optional) "I Walked Today Where Jesus Walked"

I walked today where Jesus walked in days of long ago:
I wandered down each path He knew, with rev'rent step and slow.
Those little lanes, they have not changed—a sweet peace fills the air.
I walked today where Jesus walked, and felt His presence there.

My pathway led through Bethlehem, ah mem'ries ever sweet;
The little hills of Galilee, that knew those childish feet;
The Mount of Olives: hallowed scenes that Jesus knew before;
I saw the mighty Jordan roll as in the days of yore.

I knelt today where Jesus knelt, where all alone He prayed;
The Garden of Gethsemane, my heart felt unafraid!
I picked my heavy burden up, and with Him by my side,
I climbed the Hill of Calvary, I climbed the Hill of Calvary,
I climbed the Hill of Calvary, where on the cross He died!
I walked today where Jesus walked, and felt Him close to me![1]

Scripture Reading:

"He who dwells in the shelter of the Most High, who abides in the shadow of the Almighty, will say to the Lord, 'My refuge and my fortress; my God, in whom I trust.' For he will deliver you from the snare of the fowler and from the deadly pestilence; he will cover you with his pinions, and under his wings you will find refuge; his faithfulness is a shield and buckler" (Psalm 91:1–4).

"Wait for the Lord; be strong, and let your heart take courage; yea, wait for the Lord!" (Psalm 27:14).

"The Lord is good, a stronghold in the day of trouble; he knows those who take refuge in him" (Nahum 1:7).

"If we live, we live to the Lord, and if we die, we die to the Lord; so then, whether we live or whether we die, we are the Lord's. For to this end Christ died and lived again, that he might be Lord both of the dead and of the living" (Romans 14:8–9).

"While he was still speaking, there came from the ruler's house some who said, 'Your daughter is dead. Why trouble the Teacher any further?' But ignoring what they said, Jesus said to the ruler of the synagogue, 'Do not fear, only believe.' And he allowed no one to follow him except Peter and James and John the brother of James. When they came to the house of the ruler of the synagogue, he saw a tumult, and people

[1] Poem by Daniel S. Twohig, music by Geoffrey O'Hara, published by G. Schirmer, Inc. Copyright, 1937. Reprinted by permission.

weeping and wailing loudly. And when he had entered, he said to them, 'Why do you make a tumult and weep? The child is not dead but sleeping.' And they laughed at him. But he put them all outside, and took the child's father and mother and those who were with him, and went in where the child was. Taking her by the hand he said to her, 'Talitha cumi'; which means, 'Little girl, I say to you, arise.' And immediately the girl got up and walked; for she was twelve years old. And immediately they were overcome with amazement. And he strictly charged them that no one should know this, and told them to give her something to eat" (Mark 5:35–43).

Prayer:

O Thou who art nigh unto the afflicted and with tender compassion healest the brokenhearted, hear Thou our prayer. Though we cannot understand the mystery of death nor all that happens in our journey toward eternity, yet we know that Thou art all-wise, and we have the assurance that Thou dost work in all things for good to them that love Thee. Grant that none will become bitter and hardened by this experience; rather fill our minds with love and good will.

We thank Thee, our Father, for the sweet life, kind and true, innocent and genuine, courteous and thoughtful, sincere and radiant, that made this one, now asleep in Jesus, so beloved by all.

Help us to be inspired by her example, and to exemplify her childlike faith and sincerity that we might follow in the footsteps of the Redeemer. Give us the inward traits that made her beautiful and strong—the hope that kept her loyal, the love that made her sweet, the faith that made her pure.

Console with Thy mercy all who were precious to her, and unto whom she was dear. Open their eyes to see the Father's

house on high, and may they feel assured that the departed
has found a better life, and a more perfect circumstance.
May this visitation of death quicken in us a truer and holier
life in our souls. In the name of Jesus Christ. Amen.

Meditation:

GATHERING OF GOD'S JEWELS

E. L. Godkin, once editor of the *New York Evening Post*,
after the death of his young daughter wrote: "When my
little darling left her father's house for the last time last Fri-
day, I felt assured that somewhere, a wise and better Father
awaited her, and that, in His care, she would one day become all—more than all—that I rashly and fondly hoped to
see her in mine."[2]

She was the kind of girl that God seeks and wants in His
eternal kingdom. The prophet Malachi described such a one
in these words, "They shall be mine, saith the Lord of hosts,
in that day when I make up my jewels" (Malachi 3:17, AV).
Many times have I heard this girl referred to as a real
"jewel." Like a diamond with its flashing lustre, so her soul
reflected the love of Jesus and the Christian graces. The fac-
ets of love, sincerity, brotherliness, generosity, spirituality
made her a jewel of God. He has called her to be one of His.

From RESIGNATION

There is no death! What seems so is transition.
　　This life of mortal breath
Is but a suburb of the life elysian,
　　Whose portal we call Death.

She is not dead—the child of our affection,
　　But gone unto that school
Where she no longer needs our poor protection,
　　And Christ Himself doth rule.

In that great cloister's stillness and seclusion,
  By guardian angels led,
Safe from temptation, safe from sin's pollution.
  She lives, whom we call dead.

Day after day we think what she is doing
  In those bright realms of air;
Year after year her tender steps pursuing,
  Behold her grown more fair.

Thus do we walk with her, and keep unbroken
  The bond which nature gives,
Thinking that our remembrance, though unspoken,
  May reach her where she lives.

Not as a child shall we again behold her;
  For when with raptures wild
In our embraces we again enfold her,
  She will not be a child.

But a fair maiden, in her Father's mansion,
  Clothed with celestial grace;
And beautiful with all the soul's expansion,
  Shall we behold her face.[3]

In the Scriptures (Matthew 9:18–26) we read of the
ruler whose daughter was dead. The palace was filled with
professional mourners and unusual grief. When Jesus entered He said, "Depart; for the girl is not dead but sleepeth."
To Jesus death was an easy and quiet thing. Such a concept
of death is easily pictured. A mother sits with her child upon
her knee. Though tired with the day's romp and play, the
child feebly tries to beat back the descending atmosphere
of sleep. But a larger wisdom presses her eyelids down and
caught unaware the little one relaxes and slips gently out
upon a sea of dreams. The mother lays her little one down
upon the bed and she wakes at the dawn of a new day. We

are but children of a larger growth, fighting against the last great sleep so that we may enjoy the material things of life. It is a futile fight—for all the treasures such as money, homes, friends and children must be left behind. A larger wisdom presses our eyelids down. Strong arms lay us away. A great love gives peace, and we rise in a newness of life in another world.

"But we would not have you ignorant, brethren, concerning those who are asleep," says Paul, the Apostle, "that you may not grieve as others do who have no hope. For since we believe that Jesus died and rose again, even so, through Jesus, God will bring with him those who have fallen asleep" (I Thessalonians 4:13–14).

Hymn: (Optional) "Lead, Kindly Light"

> Lead, kindly Light, amid th'encircling gloom,
>   Lead Thou me on!
> The night is dark, and I am far from home;
>   Lead Thou me on!
> Keep Thou my feet; I do not ask to see
> The distant scene—one step enough for me.
>
> I was not ever thus, nor prayed that Thou
>   Shouldst lead me on;
> I loved to choose and see my path; but now
>   Lead Thou me on!
> I loved the garish day, and, spite of fears,
> Pride ruled my will; remember not past years.
>
> So long Thy power hath blest me, sure it still
>   Will lead me on,
> O'er moor and fen, o'er crag and torrent, till
>   The night is gone;
> And with the morn those angel faces smile;
> Which I have loved long since, and lost awhile![4]

Benediction:

"Now may our Lord Jesus Christ himself, and God our Father, who loved us and gave us eternal comfort and good hope through grace, comfort your hearts and establish them in every good work and word" (II Thessalonians 2:16–17).

Postlude:

"Oh, Jesus I Have Promised"
"Jesus, Lover of My Soul"

V

For a Teen-Age Youth

Prelude:

"In the Hour of Trial"
"Finlandia"

Opening Scriptural Sentence:

"I lift up my eyes to the hills. From whence does my help come? My help comes from the Lord, who made heaven and earth" (Psalm 121:1–2).

Invocation:

"O Holy Father, whose mercies are everlasting to everlasting, to Thee do we fly for refuge in our affliction. From the grief that burdens our spirits, from the sense of solitude and loss, from the doubts and fainting of the soul in its trouble, we turn to Thee. Strengthen our feeble faith, we

implore Thee: comfort our hearts, and by the gospel of Thy
beloved Son speak peace to our souls, through Jesus Christ.
Amen."[1]

Hymn: (Optional) "O Love That Wilt Not Let Me Go"

   (This may be organ music, choral anthem, vocal solo, or
spoken)

> O Love that wilt not let me go,
> I rest my weary soul in Thee;
> I give Thee back the life I owe,
> That in Thine ocean depths its flow
> May richer, fuller be.
>
> O Light that followest all my way,
> I yield my flickering torch to Thee;
> My heart restores its borrowed ray,
> That in Thy sunshine's blaze its day
> May brighter, fairer be.
>
> O Joy that seekest me through pain,
> I cannot close my heart to Thee;
> I trace the rainbow through the rain,
> And feel the promise is not vain
> That morn shall tearless be.
>
> O Cross that liftest up my head,
> I dare not ask to fly from Thee;
> I lay in dust life's glory dead,
> And from the ground there blossoms red
> Life that shall endless be.[2]

Scripture Reading:

   "And I tell you, Ask, and it will be given you; seek, and
you will find; knock, and it will be opened to you. For every
one who asks receives, and he who seeks finds, and to him
who knocks it will be opened. What father among you, if
his son asks for a fish, will instead of a fish give him a ser-

pent; or if he asks for an egg, will give him a scorpion? If you then, who are evil, know how to give good gifts to your children, how much more will the heavenly Father give the Holy Spirit to those who ask him?" (Luke 11:9–13).

"How can a young man keep his way pure? By guarding it according to thy word. With my whole heart I seek thee; let me not wander from thy commandments! I have laid up thy word in my heart, that I might not sin against thee. Blessed be thou, O Lord; teach me thy statutes! With my lips I declare all the ordinances of thy mouth. In the way of thy testimonies I delight as much as in all riches. I will meditate on thy precepts, and fix my eyes on thy ways. I will delight in thy statutes; I will not forget thy word" (Psalm 119: 9–16).

"Soon afterward he went to a city called Nain, and his disciples and a great crowd went with him. As he drew near to the gate of the city, behold, a man who had died was being carried out, the only son of his mother, and she was a widow; and a large crowd from the city was with her. And when the Lord saw her, he had compassion on her and said to her, 'Do not weep.' And he came and touched the bier, and the bearers stood still. And he said, 'Young man, I say to you, arise.' And the dead man sat up, and began to speak. And he gave him to his mother" (Luke 7:11–15).

Meditation:

THE ACCOMPLISHMENT OF YOUTH

Dwight L. Moody said at Henry Drummond's death, "The home-going of Drummond adds one more attraction to heaven." So the home-going of this youth adds one more attraction to heaven.

I cannot say, and I will not say
That he is dead. He is just away.

With a cheery smile, and a wave of the hand,
He has wandered into an unknown land.

And left us dreaming how very fair
It needs must be since he lingers there.

And you—O you, who the wildest yearn
For the old-time step and the glad return—

Think of him faring on, as dear
In the love of there as the love of here;

Think of him, still as the same, I say;
He is not dead—he is just away![3]

"He had not lived in vain" was the response of a searching father concerning the death of his teen-age son. How could a father say that the boy had not lived in vain, when he was taken at such a tender age? How could a father not be bitter and resentful when it seemed the lad had everything for which to live?

Jesus, who also died at a seemingly untimely and premature age, gave the clue when He said, ". . . I have finished the work which thou gavest me to do" (John 17:4). He accomplished in His short life and by His death what God intended Him to accomplish, something He could never have attained any other way. His untimely and unjust death brought men face to face with a cosmic power; it jarred those calloused in conscience; it spoke the message of the heart.

I

This boy's life was not in vain, because he *opened our lives to happiness and to God*. We question why a young

man of these ideals should be taken at such an age. It is
not for us to understand now; however, he has probably
lived more in his few years than many people do in scores
of years. His influence for good and for Christ was far beyond his number of years. Science has learned to preserve
and lengthen life, but there is no virtue in long years if one
has not learned how to live. Quality is more important than
quantity. Many have died at early ages; nonetheless their
dedication has profoundly affected multitudes.

> We live in deeds, not years; in thoughts, not breaths;
> In feelings, not in figures on a dial.
> We should count time by heart-throbs. He most lives
> Who thinks most, feels the noblest, acts the best.

> * * *

> Life's but a means unto an end: that end,
> Beginning, mean, and end to all things—God.[4]

How sad life would have been for the parents without this
boy. He brought smiles, joy, and happiness. How dry and
weary life would be without children and youth—it would
be like a day without a morning, or a year without a spring.

How selfish we can become without someone to care for
but ourselves. When a child and youth come into a home,
what possibilities of service, or unselfish devotion, of sacrifice, or character building. We need for our own spirits,
what caring for children can do to us. We talk about educat-
ing our children; they educate us! Children bring to development our better natures. Many a parent had never given
God a place in his thinking or loyalty, until a child was born.
Who can measure the influence of youth? How often it is
that the idealism, vision, sacrifice, enthusiasm, and sincerity
of youth puts us to shame, constantly challenging our status
quo. Sometimes the posthumous influence is greater by dy-

ing than living. Think of Joan of Arc, who in her teens defied the corruptness of her day by courageously laying down her life, but in so doing she shook the world and is remembered in honor to this day. Think of the death of Arthur Henry Hallam that inspired Tennyson to write "In Memoriam," thus to bless all posterity.

Grace Coolidge, wife of the former president, felt this way about her son five years after his death when she penned "The Open Door":

> You, my son,
> Have shown me God.
> Your kiss upon my cheek
> Has made me feel the gentle touch
> Of Him who leads us on.
> The memory of your smile, when young,
> Reveals His face,
> As mellowing years come on apace.
> And when you went before,
> You left the gates of heaven ajar
> That I might glimpse,
> Approaching from afar,
> The glories of His grace.
> Hold, son, my hand,
> Guide me along the path,
> That, coming,
> I may stumble not,
> Nor roam,
> Nor fail to show the way
> Which leads us home.[5]

II

This boy's life will not be in vain, if we *dedicate ourselves to completing his unfulfilled dreams.* During World War II, Dr. William Tyson was called to see a young mother who had received word that her husband had been killed in the Battle of the Bulge. He went to comfort her. As he was leaving she turned to a boy, barely three years old, who was playing. "That's our only child," she said. "He looks just like Joe." A sob came from her shocked and broken heart. Then a light seemed to illumine her face. "You know," she continued, "Joe will always be alive. As long as little Joe and I keep alive the memory in the things he believed in and stood for, Joe will live. He will never die. Little Joe and I won't let him die."[6]

One is constantly impressed with the uncertainty of life. Family Bibles all over the land contain inscriptions: "Born 1924—died 1944"; "Born 1930—died 1951"; "Born 1940 —died 1958"—young men with lives cut short and dreams of peace unrealized. This young man had dreams of a better world, a warless, just society—these yearnings sought expression. Let us devote our lives to fulfilling these causes in such a way that he will not have lived in vain.

A beautiful Chinese Christian girl was being put to death at the stake during the Boxer Rebellion in the late 1800's for failure to compromise principles. Her relatives and friends gathered about weeping for her. It is recorded that, from the already lighted fagots, she said in a clear voice words which are prophetic for us this day, "Do not weep for me. I am dying for a great cause. What are you living for?"

Prayer:

"Come to thy servants, most merciful God, in their sore need, and though they may not fathom Thy vast designs, temper their sorrow with gratitude. Turn their thoughts from that which is lost to that which they can never lose, to the radiant charm of youth, to the undying influence of maturing powers, that these sanctifying memories may be to them as a garment of praise for the spirit of heaviness, and beyond these intimate consolations, add a clearer discernment of the meaning of life; not in its duration but in its inspiration; not in the number of its years but in the timelessness of its integrity and charm; that the great words may be spoken again in their hearts; he having lived a short time has fulfilled a long time, and youth soon perfected rebukes the many years of the unrighteous. Set before them the appealing figure of the young Jesus, with His work, as it seemed, unfinished and His life prematurely and tragically lost; and let them hear His unperturbed and tranquillizing message: 'Peace I leave with you; my peace I give unto you. I have finished the work which was given me to do.' " Amen.[7]

Hymn: (Optional) "Guide Me, O Thou Great Jehovah"

> Guide me, O Thou great Jehovah, Pilgrim through
>   this barren land;
> I am weak, but Thou are mighty, Hold me with
>   Thy powerful hand;
> Bread of heaven, Bread of heaven,
>   Feed me till I want no more.
>
> Open now the crystal fountain, Whence the
>   healing stream doth flow;
> Let the fire and cloudy pillar Lead me all my
>   journey through;
> Strong Deliverer, Strong Deliverer,
>   Be Thou still my strength and shield.
>
> When I tread the verge of Jordan, Bid my
>   anxious fears subside;
> Bear me through the swelling current; Land
>   me safe on Canaan's side;
> Songs of praises, Songs of praises,
>   I will ever give to Thee.[8]

Benediction:

The peace of our Lord Jesus Christ be with you. Amen.

Postlude:

"Faith" (Mendelssohn)

"Abide With Me"

"Elegy" (Franz Schubert)

VI

For a Youth in Military Service

Prelude:

"When Thou Art Near" (Bach)

"Jesus, Still Lead On" (L. Carwall)

"What a Friend We Have in Jesus"

Opening Scriptural Sentence:

"Be strong and of good courage . . . be not frighte
neither be dismayed; for the Lord your God is with
wherever you go" (Joshua 1:6, 9).

Invocation:

Our loving Father, who art from everlasting to ever
ing, look tenderly upon us in our sorrow, abide with u
our loneliness, lift upon us the light of Thy countena
and grant us Thy peace—through Jesus Christ the Princ
Peace and conqueror of death. Amen.

Hymn: (Optional) "There Is No Death"

(This may be organ music, choral anthem, vocal sol
spoken)

I tell you they have not died,
　　They live and breathe with you;
They walk here at your side,
　　They tell you things are true.
Why dream of poppied sod
　　When you can feel their breath,
When flow'r and soul and God
　　Knows there is no death?

Death's but an open door,
　　We move from room to room,
There is one life, no more;
　　No dying and no tomb
Why seek ye them above,
　　Those that ye love dear?
The All of God is Love,
　　The All of God is Here.

I tell you they have not died,
　　Their hands clasp yours and mine;
They are but glorified,
　　They have become divine.
They live! they know! they see!
　　They shout with every breath
"Life is eternity
　　There is no death!"[1]

Scripture Reading:

"Thou turnest man back to the dust, and sayest, 'Turn back, O children of men!' For a thousand years in thy sight are but as yesterday when it is past, or as a watch in the night. Thou dost sweep men away; they are like a dream, like grass which is renewed in the morning: in the morning it flourishes and is renewed; in the evening it fades and withers" (Psalm 90:3–6).

"Strengthen the weak hands, and make firm the feeble knees. Say to those who are of a fearful heart, 'Be strong, fear not! Behold, your God will come with vengeance, with the recompense of God. He will come and save you.' Then the eyes of the blind shall be opened, and the ears of the deaf unstopped; then shall the lame man leap like a hart, and the tongue of the dumb sing for joy. For waters shall break forth in the wilderness, and streams in the desert; the burning sand shall become a pool, and the thirsty ground springs of water; the haunt of jackals shall become a swamp, the grass shall become reeds and rushes. And a highway shall be there, and it shall be called the Holy Way; the unclean shall not pass over it, and fools shall not err therein. No lion shall be there, nor shall any ravenous beast come up on it; they shall not be found there, but the redeemed shall walk there. And the ransomed of the Lord shall return, and come to Zion with singing, with everlasting joy upon their heads; they shall obtain joy and gladness, and sorrow and sighing shall flee away" (Isaiah 35:3–10).

"For I am already on the point of being sacrificed; the time of my departure has come. I have fought the good fight, I have finished the race, I have kept the faith. Henceforth there is laid up for me the crown of righteousness, which the Lord, the righteous judge, will award to me on that Day, and not only to me but also to all who have loved his appearing" (II Timothy 4:6–8).

HOW BEAUTIFUL TO BE WITH GOD

How beautiful to be with God,
When earth is fading like a dream,
And from this mist-encircled shore
We launch upon the unknown stream.

No doubt, no fear, no anxious care,
But comforted by staff and rod,
In the faith-brightened hour of death
How beautiful to be with God.

> Then let it fade, this dream of earth,
>   When I have done my lifework here,
> Or long, or short, as seemeth best—
>   What matters so God's will appear.
>
> I will not fear to launch my bark,
>   Upon the darkly rolling flood,
> 'Tis but to pierce the mist—and then
>   How beautiful to be with God.[2]

Meditation:

THERE IS NO DEATH

"I am persuaded, that neither death, nor life . . . shall be able to separate us from the love of God which is in Christ Jesus our Lord" (Romans 8:38–39, AV). If we love God, then we are not separated from those who have gone on and who love Him.

The story behind Geoffrey O'Hara's "There Is No Death" comes from the field of battle.

In 1919 Gordon Johnstone met a retired Canadian Army colonel whose command had been wiped out in a series of bloody battles. At first, feeling the loss of his men, the colonel was overwhelmed with despondency. Then slowly his attitude of abject despair changed into a quiet faith in God and in eternal life. The colonel said, "I began to feel their breath, their hands touched mine as I walked down the trenches. I could hear their voices. I tell you they have not died . . . I tell you they have not died."

Something about this hard-boiled colonel's faith in the other world caused Gordon Johnstone to pen the words which Geoffrey O'Hara set to music, "There is no death." As one singer stated, "Every time I sing this song, my boy appears by my side."

Life does go on in another world—which is a place of

"many mansions," activity, democracy, freedom, joy, justice—with no more war, no cruel death, no tyrants; these were the things this boy fought for. This boy did his part; "no greater love hath any man than this." He hated war, he loved life.

We believe he has now, today, in that other world, what he deserves and fought for:

> Let them in, Peter, they are very tired;
> Give them the couches where the angels sleep.
> Let them wake whole again to new dawns fired
> With sun, not war. And may their peace be deep.
> Remember where the broken bodies lie . . .
> And give them things they like. Let them make noise.
> God knows how young they were to have to die!
> Give swing bands, not gold harps, to these our boys.
> Let them love, Peter,—they have had no time—
> Girls sweet as meadow wind, with flowering hair . . .
> They should have trees and bird song, hills to climb—
> The taste of summer in a ripened pear.
> Tell them how they are missed. Say not to fear;
> It's going to be all right with us down here.[3]

If your boy could talk with you now, he would want you to be brave, strong, and have faith in God. He would not want you to be resentful, hateful, nor fearful.

A twenty-two-year-old Dutch lad who, with his three companions, was shot to death on February 27, 1942, by a Nazi firing squad for temporarily escaping, wrote a letter to his parents containing the following statements:

Dear Father:

. . . I have been able to pray much, and have the firm conviction that I may look forward to a death in Christ. In a little while at five o'clock it is going to happen and that is not so terrible. It is, after all, only one moment, and then I shall be with

God—no more terrible miseries and the sadness of the earth. Is that, after all, such a dreadful transition?

On the contrary, it is beautiful to be in God's strength. God has told us that He will not forsake us if only we pray to Him for support. I feel so strongly my nearness to God, I am fully prepared to die. I hope that will be a consolation to you.

I know quite well that it is horrible. We are still so young. But God knows that our cause was a just one. I think it is much worse for you than for me, because I know that I have confessed all my sins to Him and have become very quiet. Therefore, do not mourn, but trust in God and pray for strength.

Mother, dear mother . . . do not cry, darling. Be courageous. . . . Father . . . be strong in your belief which I know you have like Mother. Do not mourn, but thank God that we may have the certainty of His grace. . . .

Greet everybody, for us. . . . We are courageous. Be the same. They can only take our bodies. Our souls are in God's hands. That should be sufficient consolation. . . .

Have no hate. I die without hatred. . . . I am going—until we meet again in a reunion which will be so much happier. May God bless you all. Kees.[4]

Prayer:

O thou who makest no life in vain, and who lovest all that Thou hast made, keep in tender love the life which we shall hold in blessed memory. We thank Thee for the rich contribution this young man made to our lives, to our nation, and the Kingdom of God. We are grateful for his ideals, his convictions, his faith. We commend him to Thy infinite, loving care, confident in the promise of everlasting life which Thou hast given to all who believe in Jesus Christ, Thy Son.

Grant us now the depth of faith to leave with Thee his keeping, the inward strength to face our tomorrows, the moral courage to fulfill his noblest dreams and unfulfilled work, and the spiritual discipline that finds us ready for life's closing tide. Amen.

Benediction:

"Now unto the King eternal, immortal, invisible, the only wise God, be honour and glory for ever and ever. Amen" (I Timothy 1:17, AV).

Postlude:

"Lead On, O King Eternal"

VII

For a Young Mother

Prelude:

"Traumerei" (Robert Schumann)
"What a Friend We Have in Jesus"

Opening Scriptural Sentence:

"Our help is in the name of the Lord, who made heaven and earth" (Psalm 124:8). "And now has manifested through the appearance of our Savior Christ Jesus who abolished death and brought life and immortality to light through the gospel" (II Timothy 1:10).

Invocation:

Eternal Spirit, in whom life is our joy and death only an incident in our eternal adventure, lift our eyes beyond the shadows of the earth and enable us to put our trust in Thee —we pray in the name of Jesus. Amen.

Hymn: (Optional) "O for a Faith That Will Not Shrink"
  (This may be organ music, choral anthem, vocal solo, **or** spoken)

> O for a faith that will not shrink,
> Though pressed by every foe
> That will not tremble on the brink
> Of any earthly woe!
>
> That will not murmur or complain
> Beneath the chastening rod,
> But, in the hour of grief or pain,
> Will lean upon its God.
>
> A faith that shines more bright and clear
> When tempests rage without,
> That when in danger knows no fear,
> In darkness feels no doubt;
>
> Lord, give us such a faith as this,
> And then, whate'er may come,
> We'll taste e'en here the hallowed bliss
> Of the eternal home.[1]

Scripture Reading:

  "Now if Christ is preached as raised from the dead, how can some of you say that there is no resurrection of the dead? . . . If Christ has not been raised, your faith is futile and you are still in your sins. . . . If in this life we who are in Christ have only hope, we are of all men most to be pitied. But in fact Christ has been raised from the dead, the first fruits of those who have fallen asleep. For as by a man came death, by a man has come also the resurrection of the dead. For as in Adam all die, so also in Christ shall all be made alive. . . . But some one will ask, 'How are the dead raised? With what kind of body do they come?' You foolish

man! What you sow does not come to life unless it dies. A
what you sow is not the body which is to be, but a bare k
nel, perhaps of wheat or of some other grain. But God gi
it a body as he has chosen, and to each kind of seed its c
body. For not all flesh is alike, but there is one kind for m
another for animals, another for birds, and another for f
There are celestial bodies and there are terrestrial bod
but the glory of the celestial is one, and the glory of the
restrial is another. There is one glory of the sun, and
other glory of the moon, and another glory of the stars;
star differs from star in glory. So is it with the resurrect
of the dead. What is sown is perishable, what is raised
imperishable. It is sown in dishonor, it is raised in glory
is sown in weakness, it is raised in power. It is sown a ph
cal body, it is raised a spiritual body. If there is a physi
body, there is also a spiritual body. Thus it is written, 'T
first man Adam became a living being'; the last Adam
came a life-giving spirit. But it is not the spiritual which
first but the physical, and then the spiritual. The first n
was from the earth, a man of dust; the second man is fr
heaven. As was the man of dust, so are those who are of
dust; and as is the man of heaven, so are those who are
heaven. Just as we have borne the image of the man of d
we shall also bear the image of the man of heaven. I tell y
this, brethren; flesh and blood cannot inherit the kingd
of God, nor does the perishable inherit the imperishal
Lo! I tell you a mystery. We shall not all sleep, but we sh
all be changed, in a moment, in the twinkling of an eye,
the last trumpet. For the trumpet will sound, and the de
will be raised imperishable, and we shall be changed. I
this perishable nature must put on the imperishable, a
this mortal nature must put on immortality. When the p
ishable puts on the imperishable, and the mortal puts

immortality, then shall come to pass the saying that is written: 'Death is swallowed up in victory. O death, where is thy victory? O death, where is thy sting?' The sting of death is sin, and the power of sin is the law. But thanks be to God, who gives us the victory through our Lord Jesus Christ. Therefore, my beloved brethren, be steadfast, immovable, always abounding in the work of the Lord, knowing that in the Lord, your labor is not in vain" (I Corinthians 15:12, 17, 19–22, 35–58).

Prayer:

Almighty God our Father, from whom we have come and unto whom we return, in whom we live and move and have our being: we praise Thee this day for the gospel which brings hope in time of despair. For the good life of the departed, her faith, her home, her loyalty, her ideals—wherein there was virtue—we praise Thee, O God. We hold in sacred and tender memory this mother.

Thou who can turn the shadows of night into morning, and who art a refuge for Thy children in their affliction, comfort we pray these upon whom this death so closely falls. Enable them to find in Thee strength, to know the love of Christ which passes all understanding, to believe with confidence in the reality of the unseen—then we know truly the sting of death will be taken away.

Enable us all to be inspired by the example of those who have gone before, that we may run with patience the race that is set before us, looking unto Jesus, so that when this changeful life shall have passed away, we may meet with those whom Thou hast loved in the Kingdom of glory. So let a portion of this mother's believing, loving, persevering spirit abide with us to the end, in the name of Jesus Christ, our Lord. Amen.

Hymn: (Optional) "Build Thee More Stately Mansions"
   (This may be solo or choral anthem)

> Build thee more stately mansions, O my soul,
>   As the swift seasons roll!
>   Leave thy low-vaulted past!
> Let each new temple, nobler than the last,
> Shut thee from heaven with a dome more vast,
>   Till thou at length are free,
> Leaving thine outgrown shell by life's unresting sea.[2]

Meditation:

IRREPRESSIBLE HOPE

We are always saddened when death invades a family circle, and quite naturally so. It is human to love the handclasp, the light of trusting eyes, and the sound of a cheerful voice. With Tennyson we beg, "O for the touch of a vanished hand, and the sound of a voice that is still." We are saddened because of our loneliness, our fears, our uncertainties. However, this day let us turn our fear into faith, our sorrow into joy, our doubt into certainty, our loneliness into Divine companionship.

Paul, the saintly Apostle with a pastor's heart, said, "[Do] not grieve as others do who have no hope" (I Thessalonians 4:13). If we were without hope, we might mourn. If we had no Christian faith, we might despair in melancholy. But the very essence of the Christian religion is hope, hope irrepressible.

Hope is the blessed anticipation that fills the heart with gladness. Hope is the Christian expectation of eternal good. Hope is toiling through long days with a look to some enchanted evening. Hope is Shelley singing with the night, "If winter comes, can spring be far behind?" Hope is a pilgrimage, punctuated at the end by a light in the window of home. Hope is one of the everlastings, traveling in a great company with faith on the left and love on the right: "Now abideth faith, hope and love" (I Corinthians 13:13). Faith is empty and love is meaningless without hope. Hope is an anchor of the soul. Hope steadies us in storms, holds us up, gives us a spirit which is undefeatable. When hope vanishes, there is grieving, for all has vanished. When hope is alive, all things are alive.

Today, though we stand in the valley of the shadow of death, yet we stand in the light of the greatest hope in the world. Though the darkness has enveloped us, the rays of a glorious dawn are shining through. Though we stand in the presence of death, yet we stand on the threshold of life. Shortly before his death Dwight L. Moody said, "Some day you will read that D. L. Moody is dead. Don't believe it. At that moment I shall be more alive than I am now." There is a bronze statue outside the Hall of Archives in Washington, D.C. that has a young girl on a chair, leafing through a book. The girl is turning the last page, but on the inscription beneath the statue are these words, "All that is past is Prologue." That composes our Christian hope. Earthly life is just a prologue to something great and wonderful.

But you say, you cannot prove it. We cannot prove it by scientific logic, but we can by hope—that intimation of the human soul which is the more profound source of confidence. It has been suggested that perhaps we look at death as an unborn child might look at birth. Snuggled beneath its mother's heart, the child is protected and warm. If it could take voice, it might say, "I don't want to be born. I am happy here. I am afraid of birth." In those prenatal days, it might regard birth as we do death. It is the end of one certain experience and the beginning of an uncertain one. But then the child is born; there it sees the kindest, sweetest face in the world. There it is cuddled in loving arms; there it is able to develop and grow, work and serve. It is a happy experience. Should we fear death, which is a birth into another world? Should we be terrified at the experience? Would we deny our beloved the privilege of existence in another realm?

AN EPITAPH

Let us not think of our departed dead
    As caught and cumbered in their graves of earth;
    But think of death as of another birth,
As a new freedom for the wings outspread,
A new adventure waiting on ahead,
    As a new joy of more ethereal mirth,
    As a new world with friends of nobler worth,
Where all may taste a more immortal bread.
So, comrades, if you pass my grave sometime,
Pause long enough to breath this little rhyme:
    "Here now the dust of Edwin Markham lies,
But lo, he is not here; he is afar
    On life's great errands under mightier skies,
And pressing on toward some melodious star."[3]

"[Do] not grieve as others do who have no hope"—but:

So live, that when thy summons comes to join
The innumerable caravan, which moves
To that mysterious realm, where each shall take
His chamber in the silent halls of death,
Thou go not, like the quarry-slave at night,
Scourged to his dungeon, but, sustained and soothed
By an unfaltering trust, approach thy grave
Like one who wraps the drapery of his couch
About him, and lies down to pleasant dreams.[4]

Benediction:

"Grace be unto you, and peace, from God our Father, and from the Lord Jesus Christ" (I Corinthians 1:3, AV).

Postlude:

"I Waited for the Lord" (Mendelssohn)

VIII
For One in Middle Age

Prelude:

"O Sacred Head Now Wounded" (Brahms)

Opening Scriptural Sentence:

(Congregation in unison or by minister)

"The Lord is my shepherd, I shall not want; he makes me lie down in green pastures. He leads me beside still waters; he restores my soul. He leads me in paths of righteousness for his name's sake. Even though I walk through the valley of the shadow of death, I fear no evil; for thou art with me; thy rod and thy staff, they comfort me. Thou preparest a table before me in the presence of my enemies; thou anointest my head with oil, my cup overflows. Surely goodness and mercy shall follow me all the days of my life; and I shall dwell in the house of the Lord for ever" (Psalm 23).

Invocation:

O God of Peace, who hast taught us that in quietness and confidence shall be our strength; by the might of Thy Spirit lift us, we pray Thee, to Thy presence, where we may be still and know that Thou art God, through Jesus Christ our Lord. Amen.

Hymn: (Optional) "How Firm a Foundation, Ye Saints of the Lord"

(This may be organ music, choral anthem, vocal solo, or spoken)

> How firm a foundation, ye saints of the Lord,
> Is laid for your faith in His excellent word!
> What more can He say than to you He hath said,
> To you who for refuge to Jesus have fled?
>
> "Fear not, I am with thee, O be not dismayed;
> For I am thy God, I will still give thee aid;
> I'll strengthen thee, help thee, and cause thee to stand,
> Upheld by my righteous, omnipotent hand.
>
> "When through the deep waters I call thee to go,
> The rivers of sorrow shall not overflow;
> For I will be near thee, thy troubles to bless,
> And sanctify to thee thy deepest distress.
>
> "When through fiery trials thy pathway shall lie,
> My grace, all-sufficient, shall be thy supply;
> The flame shall not hurt thee; I only design
> Thy dross to consume, and thy gold to refine.
>
> "The soul that on Jesus hath leaned for repose,
> I will not, I will not desert to his foes;
> That soul though all hell should endeavor to shake,
> I'll never, no never, no never forsake." Amen.

Scripture Reading:

"O Lord, who shall sojourn in thy tent? Who shall dwell on thy holy hill? He who walks blamelessly, and does what is right, and speaks truth from his heart; who does not slander with his tongue, and does no evil to his friend, nor takes up a reproach against his neighbor; in whose eyes a reprobate is despised, but who honors those who fear the Lord; who swears to his own hurt and does not change; who does not put out his money at interest, and does not take a bribe against the innocent. He who does these things shall never be moved" (Psalm 15).

"After this I looked, and behold, a great multitude which no man could number, from every nation, from all tribes and peoples and tongues, standing before the throne and before the Lamb, clothed in white robes, with palm branches in their hands, and crying out with a loud voice, 'Salvation belongs to our God who sits upon the throne, and to the Lamb!' And all the angels stood round the throne and round the elders and the four living creatures, and they fell on their faces before the throne and worshiped God, saying, 'Amen! Blessing and glory and wisdom and thanksgiving and honor and power and might be to our God for ever and ever; Amen.' Then one of the elders addressed me, saying, 'Who are these, clothed in white robes, and whence have they come?' I said to him, 'Sir, you know.' And he said to me, 'These are they who have come out of the great tribulation; they have washed their robes and made them white in the blood of the Lamb. Therefore are they before the throne of God, and serve him day and night within his temple; and he who sits upon the throne will shelter them with his presence. They shall hunger no more, neither thirst any more; the sun shall not strike them, nor any scorching heat. For the Lamb in the midst of the throne will be their shepherd, and he will guide them to springs of living water; and God will wipe away every tear from their eyes'" (Revelation 7: 9–17).

Prayer:

O Thou, who amid the changes of mortal life art ever the same, we thank Thee for the assurance that to depart and be with Christ is far better than anything this earth has to offer, and that to be absent from the body is to be at home with the Lord. With the light and facts of the gospel, we turn our thoughts away from the grave to Thy wondrous glory, trusting that love can never lose its own.

We praise Thee for the one in whose memory we are gathered. For the nobility of character exemplified, the breadth of sympathy practiced, the depth of convictions held, the love of family, and the devotion to Christ demonstrated—we are most grateful.

We beseech thee to bless the family that is severed. May the memory of this life strengthen their hope, faith, and love. Grant them the courage to return to their home and work, to discharge their duties with fidelity to Thee and loyalty to those whose trust and affection they share, for the sake of Jesus the Christ. Amen.

Hymn: (Optional) "It Is Well with My Soul"

(This may be organ music, choral anthem, vocal solo, or spoken)

> When peace, like a river, attendeth my way,
> When sorrows like sea billows roll;
> Whatever my lot, Thou hast taught me to say,
> It is well, it is well with my soul.
>
> *Chorus:*
> It is well with my soul,
> It is well, it is well
> With my soul.

And Lord, haste the day when the faith shall be sight,
The clouds be rolled back as a scroll,
The trump shall resound and the Lord shall descend,
"Even so"—it is well with my soul.[1]

THE GAIN OF DEATH

Life is composed of opposites: daylight and dark, good and bad, health and sickness, pleasure and pain, joy and sorrow. To get the full capacity of the organ, the black keys must be played as well as the white. Tears are always locked in the happiest smiles. George Matheson was motivated by such faith when he wrote:

> O joy, that seekest me through pain,
>   I cannot close my heart to Thee;
> I trace the rainbow through the rain,
> And feel the promise is not vain,
>   That morn shall tearless be.[2]

The Apostle Paul, though he loved life with its adventure, thrill, challenge, and purpose, had a desire to depart and be with Christ. He knew it would be far better and sincerely stated, "For to me . . . to die is gain" (Philippians 1:21). It was the assurance that springs from the first part of the text, "For to me to live is Christ. . . ." To live as Christ is to conquer death as He did.

If today we can look beyond our own loss, beyond the dreadfulness of suddenly being parted, beyond the remorse of a shortened life, to see the benefits and compensations of the eternal life, then we too can say, "To die is gain." It is not to be dreaded for:

> They have triumphed who had died;
> They have passed the porches wide,
> Leading from the House of Night
> To the splendid lawns of light.

They have won, for they have read
The bright secrets of the dead;
And they gain the deep unknown,
Hearing life's strange undertone.

In the race across the days
They are victors; theirs the praise,
Theirs the glory and the pride—
They have triumphed, having died![3]

It is said that when Henry Ward Beecher was on his deathbed, he suddenly rose up and said to his friend, "Just think, Pond, in a few minutes I will see Jesus." That is the desire of every Christian! Death is a glad reunion of saints, of friends, of families. Heaven, in my opinion, is not a drab place of inactivity and unreality. It is a place of consciousness, recognition, fellowship, activity. Heaven is a place so wonderful that it is beyond our ability to describe and stretches beyond our comprehension. Death is the door through which we enter such a life of blessedness: "Eye hath not seen, nor ear heard, neither have entered into the heart of man, the things which God hath prepared for them that love him" (I Corinthians 2:9, AV).

In the early days of the church, Christians were persecuted and thrown into the arena to be devoured by hungry lions. Nero, the conceited emperor, watched from the Colosseum. As the Christians knelt in prayer, looking heavenward, a strange light showed on their faces. The hilarious Nero cried out, "What are they looking at? What do they see?" Another reverently answered, "The resurrection of Jesus." Jesus Christ, though He died, and was buried, lived to be seen by several hundred people on many different occasions, and declared, ". . . because I live, you will live also." Ah, it is not loss, but gain to die.

Dwight L. Moody, upon hearing of the death of Henry Drummond, said, "The home-going of Drummond has added another attraction to heaven." So today, there has been added another attraction, a new impulse, a firmer resolve for each of us to make heaven our home.

Will Rogers felt something like that when he wrote a foreword to the book *Trails Plowed Under* by Charles Russell, who died before the book was published. In this "Letter to Charley," Will said:

You know the Big Boss gent sent a hand over and got you so quick, Charley, but I guess He needed a good man pretty bad. I knew they had been a-working shorthanded over there pretty much all the time. I guess it's hard for Him to get hold of good men; they are just getting scarce everywhere. . . . I bet you hadn't been up there three days, Charley, until you had out your pencil and was a-drawin' something funny. And I bet you that Mark Twain, and old Bill Nye, and Whitcomb Riley, and a whole bunch of those old joshers was just a-waitin' for you to pop in with all the latest ones. And I bet they are regular fellows when you meet 'em, ain't they? Most big men are. . . . When I get to thinking about all them Top Hands up there, if I could just hold a horse wrangling job with 'em, I wouldn't mind following that wagon myself. Well, you will run onto my old Dad up there, Charley, for he was a real cow hand, and I bet he is runnin' a wagon; and you will pop into some well-kept ranch house, over under some cool shady trees, and you will be asked to have dinner, and it will be the best one you ever had in your life. Well, when you are thankin' them women folks you just tell the sweet-lookin' little old lady that you knew her boy back on an outfit you used to rope for, and tell the daughters that you knew their brother, and if you see a cute little rascal runnin' round there with my brand on him, kiss him for me. Well, can't write any more, Charley, paper's all wet. It must be raining in this old bunkhouse. Of course, we're all just hangin' on here as long as we can. I don't know why we hate to go, we know it's better there. From your old friend, Will.[4]

You see, death *is* gain.

Benediction:

"To the King of ages, immortal, invisible, the only God, be honor and glory for ever and ever. Amen" (I Timothy 1:17).

Postlude:

"The Heavens Declare His Glory" (Beethoven)

IX

For an Accident Victim
(*Or Sudden Death*)

Prelude:

Prelude in E Minor (Chopin)
"What a Friend We Have in Jesus"

Opening Scriptural Sentence:

"Fear not, for I am with you, be not dismayed, for I am your God; I will strengthen you, I will help you, I will uphold you with my victorious right hand" (Isaiah 41:10).

Invocation:

Father of mercy and God of comfort, who art the author of life on both sides of death: we cast all our burdens upon Thee, assured that Thou dost care. Though life and death we do not always understand, yet Thy ways are higher than our ways, and Thy thoughts than our thoughts. So in this hour of trial, satisfy our minds, calm our spirits, and sustain us with faith, through Jesus Christ our Lord. Amen.

Hymn: (Optional) "In the Hour of Trial"
(This may be sung by congregation, choir, or as a solo)

> In the hour of trial,
> Jesus plead for me,
> Lest by base denial
> I depart from Thee;
> When Thou see'st me waver,
> With a look recall,
> Nor, for fear nor favor,
> Suffer me to fall.
>
> With forbidden pleasures
> Would this vain world charm,
> Or its sordid treasures
> Spread to work me harm;
> Bring to my remembrance
> Sad Gethsemane,
> Or, in darker semblance,
> Cross-crowned Calvary.
>
> Should Thy mercy send me
> Sorrow, toil, and woe,
> Or should pain attend me
> On my path below;
> Grant that I may never
> Fail Thy hand to see;
> Grant that I may ever
> Cast my care on Thee.[1]

(Other appropriate hymn: "Does Jesus Care?")

Scripture Reading:

"The Lord is my light and my salvation; whom shall I fear? The Lord is the stronghold of my life; of whom shall I be afraid?" (Psalm 27:1).

"Blessed be the God and Father of our Lord Jesus Christ, the Father of mercies and God of all comfort, who comforts us in all our affliction, so that we may be able to comfort those who are in any affliction, with the comfort with which we ourselves are comforted by God. For as we share abundantly in Christ's sufferings, so through Christ we share abundantly in comfort too . . . as you share in our sufferings, you will also share in our comfort" (II Corinthians 1:3–7).

"For the mountains may depart and the hills be removed, but my steadfast love shall not depart from you, and my covenant of peace shall not be removed, says the Lord, who has compassion on you" (Isaiah 54:10).

"If you love me, you will keep my commandments. And I will pray the Father, and he will give you another Counselor, to be with you for ever, even the spirit of truth, whom the world cannot receive, because it neither sees him nor knows him; you know him, for he dwells with you, and will be in you. . . . Peace I leave with you; my peace I give to you; not as the world gives do I give to you. Let not your hearts be troubled, neither let them be afraid" (John 14:15–17, 27).

Prayer:

In the solemn stillness of this hour, we raise our hearts to Thee, O God. We have talked often about Thee, but now we pray to Thee. We have read about Thee, now we lean upon Thee—trusting, believing—for there is none to whom we can turn.

We thank Thee that we have been permitted to share life until this time with *him* whom we honor and whose memory we shall forever cherish.

O Father in heaven, who art a reliever of those broken in heart and a refuge to those in trouble, bind these friends into a close bond of love and fellowship; increase their faith in the unseen and in Jesus Christ who brought immortality to light. Transform our infirmities into strength, our sins into repentance, our earthly minds into heavenly minds, our doubts into assurance—through Jesus Christ, we pray. Amen.

Meditation:

THE GOD OF COMFORT

Paul, in writing to the Corinthians long ago, said, "Blessed be God . . . the God of all comfort; Who comforteth us in all our tribulation. . . ." (II Corinthians 1:3–4, AV).

WHEN SORROW COMES

When sorrow comes, as come it must,
In God a man must put his trust.
There is no power in mortal speech
The anguish of his soul to reach,
No voice, however sweet and low,
Can comfort him or ease the blow.

He cannot from his fellow men
Take strength that will sustain him then.
With all that kindly hands will do,
And all that love may offer, too,
He must believe throughout the test
That God has willed it for the best.

We who would be his friends are dumb;
Words from our lips but feebly come;
We feel, as we extend our hands,
That one Power only understands
And truly knows the reason why
So beautiful a life must die.

We realize how helpless then
Are all the gifts of mortal men.
No words which we have power to say

Can take the sting of grief away—
That Power which marks the sparrow's fall
Must comfort and sustain us all.

When sorrow comes, as come it must,
In God a man must place his trust.
With all the wealth which he may own,
He cannot meet the test alone,
And only he may stand serene
Who has a faith on which to lean.[2]

Sorrow is universal. No one can escape it. Man is born to trouble. Job faced it long ago. He had a tremendous fortune of land holdings; he had seven sons and three daughters. He had everything—faith, fame, family, fortune, friends. Then the future changed. Enemies fell on his grazing flocks, killing the herdsmen and driving off the cattle. Fire destroyed his crops. His children were instantly killed. He was afflicted with ulcerlike sores from head to foot. He was overwhelmed with grief.

Today we face a world filled with pain, suffering, accidents, tribulation.

There is no flock, however watched and tended,
    But one dead lamb is there!
There is no fireside, howsoe'er defended
    But has one vacant chair.[3]

In such a time there is but One who can bring light out of darkness, who can heal the heart that is broken by grief, who can bring peace of soul and strength of spirit. That one is the God whom Paul called, "The God of all comfort." He did not fail Job. He did not fail Paul. He did not fail Christ. He will not fail you. When Moses bid a final fare-

    [2] From *When Day Is Done* by Edgar A. Guest, copyright 1929 by Reilly & Lee Company, Chicago, Ill. In original poem, the word "life" in last line of third stanza is "soul."

well to the Israelites, he said to them, "The eternal God is thy refuge, and underneath are the everlasting arms." "Let not your hearts be troubled; ye believe in God. . . ."

God does not give assurance against accidents, hardships, failures, trouble, or suffering. Too often, people have felt Christianity was a miracle drug to miraculously make life easy without suffering and pain. The purpose of Christianity is not to avoid difficulty, but to produce a character adequate to meet it when it comes. It does not make life easy; rather it tries to make us great enough for life. It does not give us escape from life's burdens, but strength for meeting them when they come.

The cross of Christ makes plain two facts: First, that in this world even the innocent are not exempt from suffering; and secondly, that there is a power able to surmount evil, rise above tragedy, and to comfort in the face of death. In the cross we can see God suffering with us; we see an example of triumph over agony. God puts in us a bit of Himself; He lends us reassuring powers to think; He puts love in us so we love others; He puts forgiveness in our spirit so we are not bitter; He gives us an example of how to meet suffering—and to triumph over death.

Dr. Dan Poling in his book *Faith Is Power,* tells of his son's departure for overseas duty in World War II as a chaplain. He said to his father, "Dad, I don't want you to pray for my return. It wouldn't be fair. I have no premonitions, but just don't pray for my return—just pray that I shall never be a coward; Dad, pray that I shall be adequate." Chaplain Clark Poling was one of four chaplains of three faiths to go down on the *Dorchester* which sank at 1:15 A.M. in the iceberg waters, February 5, 1943. His actions in saving lives of many men and giving away his own lifebelt make him one of the war's great heroes of courage and

Christian witness. Dr. Poling, writing of his son's death, said, "The only prayer he wanted was answered; he was adequate."[4]

May God make you adequate to face this and every trial of life.

Hymn: "Leave It There"

(This may be organ music, choral anthem, vocal solo, or spoken)

> When your enemies assail,
> And your heart begins to fail,
> Don't forget that God in heaven answers prayer;
> He will make a way for you,
> And will lead you safely thro'
> Take your burden to the Lord, and leave it there.
>
> *Chorus:*
> Leave it there, leave it there,
> Take your burden to the Lord
> And leave it there;
> If you trust and never doubt,
> He will surely bring you out;
> Take your burden to the Lord
> And leave it there.[5]

Benediction:

May Almighty God, the Father, the Son, and the Holy Spirit, bless you and keep you, now and for ever more. Amen.

Postlude:

"Through Deepening Trials" (Carless, harmonized by Schriener)
"Rock of Ages"

X

For a Cancer Victim
(*Or Any Lingering Illness*)

Prelude:

"Come, Thou Fount of Every Blessing"
"When I Survey the Wondrous Cross"
"O Sacred Head, Now Wounded"
"Beneath the Cross"

Opening Scriptural Sentence:

The invitation of the Lord is, "Come to me, all who labor and are heavy-laden, and I will give you rest. Take my yoke upon you, and learn from me; for I am gentle and lowly in heart, and you will find rest for your souls. For my yoke is easy, and my burden is light" (Matthew 11:28–30).

Invocation:

O Thou Lord of all worlds, our heavenly Father, who hast given us in Thy Son new meaning of life, new strength for weakness, new comfort for sorrow and renewed hope in time of loss—we bow before Thee. In the power of Thy Spirit, may our griefs be transformed into consolation, our infirmities into strength, our sins into repentance, and our doubts into full assurance, through Jesus Christ our Lord. Amen.

Hymn: (Optional) "I Heard the Voice of Jesus Say"

(This may be organ music, choral anthem, vocal solo, or spoken)

I heard the voice of Jesus say,
"Come unto me and rest;
Lay down, thou weary one, lay down
Thy head upon my breast."
I came to Jesus as I was,
Weary and worn and sad;
I found in Him a resting place,
And He has made me glad.

I heard the voice of Jesus say,
"Behold I freely give
The living water! thirsty one,
    stoop down, and drink, and live."
I came to Jesus, and I drank
Of that life-giving stream;
My thirst was quenched, my soul revived,
And now I live in Him.

I heard the voice of Jesus say,
"I am this dark world's light;
Look unto me, thy morn shall rise,
And all thy day be bright."
I looked to Jesus, and I found
In Him my star, my sun;
And in that light of life I'll walk,
Till traveling days are done.[1]

Scripture Reading:

"Beloved, do not be surprised at the fiery ordeal which comes upon you to prove you, as though something strange were happening to you. But rejoice in so far as you share Christ's sufferings, that you may also rejoice and be glad when his glory is revealed" (I Peter 4:12–13).

"For this slight momentary affliction is preparing for us an eternal weight of glory beyond all comparison, because we look not to the things that are seen but to the things that are unseen; for the things that are seen are transient, but the things that are unseen are eternal" (II Corinthians 4:17–18).

"I consider that the sufferings of this present time are not worth comparing with the glory that is to be revealed to us" (Romans 8:18).

"Then one of the elders addressed me, saying, 'Who are these, clothed in white robes, and whence have they come?' I said to him, 'Sir, you know.' And he said to me, 'These are they who have come out of the great tribulation: they have washed their robes, and made them white in the blood of the lamb. Therefore are they before the throne of God, and serve him day and night within his temple; and he who sits upon the throne will shelter them with his presence. They shall hunger no more, neither thirst any more; the sun shall not strike them, nor any scorching heat. For the Lamb in the midst of the throne will be their shepherd, and he will guide them to springs of living water; and God will wipe away every tear from their eyes' " (Revelation 7:13–17).

Prayer:

O Thou before whose face the generations rise and pass away, the strength of those who suffer and the repose of the one we honor, we bow before Thy presence.

We bring to Thee our words of gratitude for all the rich gifts that the departed one has brought to our life—the mutual confidence and understanding, the gift of fellowship in sharing tasks and ambitions, the joy of complete trust, the closeness of family ties.

We are thankful for *his* example and patience in suffering and for *his* uncomplaining spirit.

We thank Thee most for the assurance that death does not end life but begins a never-ending experience, which for the righteous is free from pain, suffering and fear.

O Lord, enable us to build well upon the legacy of gracious memories. Save us from weak complaint and futile regrets. Grant the family power to carry to fulfillment their joint undertakings. May their grief be transformed into consolation, their uncertainties into faith. Empower us to think and act and grow in harmony with Thy purposes and to walk in faith. Thus, may we be true to the memory of the one who has passed from our midst, and our Master, Jesus, the Christ, in whose name we pray. Amen.

Meditation:

DEATH AS A FRIEND

Death does not always appear the same. Where it lays its hand upon children or youth while in the midst of their training, it seems premature. When death snatches a middle-aged man in the prime of activity, it is an unwelcomed, dreaded guest. When death tears an infant out of the arms of its sobbing mother, it is merciless. When it reaches into a home to remove a father or mother, leaving crushing responsibilities upon the companion, death is no respecter of persons.

However, when one has lived a long, useful life, or when one has toiled through long, trying days looking to "some enchanted evening"; when one's friends and family are equally on the other side, or when illness lingers through endless days and nights and hope for recovery is gone—then death comes as an angel of mercy. It is the answer to the oft-repeated sigh, "Lord, now lettest thou thy servant depart in peace . . . For mine eyes have seen thy salvation" (Luke 2:29, 30, AV). These words were spoken originally by the patriarch, Jacob, when he had little strength in his dying body, and surely indicate to us today that to the desperate, the aged, the fearful and the incurable, death comes indeed as a friend.

Death is a friend because it brings release. After death that follows a lingering illness, it is not uncommon to hear relatives say, "Though it is hard for us, yet we know death has come as a blessing. We know it is best for her (or him)." The thought which prompts such statements is the release from sleepless nights, from agony, and long, creeping days of intense suffering.

A minister, reading the Bible to a suffering hospital patient, quoted Revelation, ". . . there shall be no more . . . sorrow, nor crying, neither shall there be any more pain. . . ." From jaws clenched in agony, came the reply, "Won't that be wonderful—no more pain!" That's why death is a friend.

It means freeing oneself from the limitations of a worn-out, diseased bodily organism and setting the spirit free for further development. It means vacating a house that has been dilapidated and ruined by storm, and moving into a large, spacious mansion with a beautiful view of the mountains and the sea. It means the transmission set is worn out and a new one must be found. It means putting off the old suit and dressing in a new, beautiful garment. It means harvesting the precious grain from a stalk bent by the last frost of fall.

Death is a friend also because it is a time of reward. Too often we think of death as coming to destroy everything for which we have lived; we should picture death as coming to save those we love. Many times we think of death as the end; rather we should think of death as the beginning of a more abundant life. We often think of losing, when it should be gain. We think of parting, instead of arrival. It is not closing the door; it is opening the gate to eternity. It is not paying a debt; it is taking a note to a bank and obtaining gold in exchange. It is not a passing to mourn; rather it is a promotion to enjoy. It is not regret; it is reward.

One man about whom I read had the right spirit, for he said to his dying mother, "I'm going to let you go now, Mother. Have a good time. You have earned this joy."

The Bible says it beautifully, "They shall hunger no more, neither thirst any more; the sun shall not strike them, nor any scorching heat. For the Lamb in the midst of the throne will be their shepherd, and he will guide them to springs of living water; and God will wipe away every tear from their eyes" (Revelation 7:16–17).

Over there all the hungers shall be satisfied, all the necessities of life met. Here people hunger. As Alfred Noyes put it, "I am full fed and yet I hunger. What means this deeper hunger of my heart?" Ah, the deep, inner, fundamental longings of the human heart are not satisfied on earth, but over there they are. In the beyond, our loved ones are protected. Here they strive for shelter and security, but over there they can sleep in perfect peace for God shall watch over them. Here their eyes are damp with tears, all life is filled with some heartbreak and disappointment; but over there, tears shall be wiped away, wrongs shall be righted, and life will be made perfect. How wonderful!

Arthur Gossip was a man who loved his wife dearly. He was left forever in the solitude of loneliness; his children were left without a mother. After this great soul contemplated her death, however, he spoke these words which have become classic: "Would you pluck the diadem from their brows again? Would you snatch the palms of victory out of her hands? Dare you compare the clumsy nothings our poor blundering love can give her here with what she must have yonder where Christ Himself has met her and heaped upon her who can think what happiness and glory?"[2] "Eye hath not seen, nor ear heard, neither have entered into the heart of man, the things which God hath prepared for them that love him."

> You are not dead—Life has but set you free!
> Your years of life were like a lovely song,
> The last sweet poignant notes of which, held long,
> Passed into silence while we listened, we
> Who loved you, listened still expectantly!
> And we about you whom you moved among
> Would feel that grief for you were surely wrong—
> You have but passed beyond where we can see.
>
> For us who knew you, dread of age is past!
> You took life, tiptoe, to the very last;
> It never lost for you its lovely look;
> You kept your interest in its thrilling book;
> To you, Death came, no conqueror, in the end—
> You merely smiled to greet another friend![3]

For, as Paul the Apostle stated, "I consider that the sufferings of this present time are not worth comparing with the glory that is to be revealed to us" (Romans 8:18).

Benediction:

"And after you have suffered a little while, the God of all grace, who has called you to his eternal glory in Christ, will himself restore, establish, and strengthen you. To him be the dominion for ever and ever." Amen (I Peter 5:10–11).

Postlude:

"Guide Me O Thou Great Jehovah"
"Wonderful Peace"

XI

For a Victim of Murder

Prelude:

"Near My God to Thee"
"The King of Love My Shepherd Is"
"I Need Thee Every Hour"

Opening Scriptural Sentence:

"The Lord is nigh unto all them that call upon him, to all that call upon him in truth" (Psalm 145:18, AV).

Invocation:

O Thou who hast never failed us nor left us alone, we believe the promises of Thy Son, our Saviour, who said, "I will not leave you comfortless . . . I will come to you." Come to us now, O Father, with Thy comforting power and spirit. Whisper to each troubled and sorrowing person the assuring words of Jesus who said to the grieved, "I am the resurrection and the life. He that believeth in me shall never die." Help us in the presence of death, to realize the reality and truth of these words, through Jesus Christ our Lord. Amen.

Hymn: (Optional) "Dear Lord and Father of Mankind"

(This may be organ music, choral anthem, congregational singing, vocal solo, quartet, or spoken)

> Dear Lord and Father of mankind,
> Forgive our foolish ways;
> Reclothe us in our rightful mind;

In purer lives Thy service find,
In deeper reverence, praise.

Drop Thy still dews of quietness,
Till all our strivings cease;
Take from our souls the strain and stress,
And let our ordered lives confess
The beauty of Thy peace.

Breathe through the heats of our desire,
Thy coolness and Thy balm;
Let sense be dumb, let flesh retire;
Speak through the earthquake, wind, and fire,
O still small voice of calm![1]

Scripture Reading:

"God is our refuge and strength, a very present help in trouble. Therefore, we will not fear, though the earth should change, though the mountains shake in the heart of the sea; though its waters roar and foam, though the mountains tremble with its tumult" (Psalm 46:1–3).

"Fear not . . . When you pass through the waters, I will be with you; and through the rivers, they shall not overwhelm you; when you walk through fire you shall not be burned, and the flame shall not consume you. For I am the Lord your God, the Holy One of Israel, your Savior" (Isaiah 43:1–3).

"My grace is sufficient for you, for my power is made perfect in weakness" (II Corinthians 12:9).

"Thou dost guide me with thy counsel, and afterward thou wilt receive me to glory. Whom have I in heaven but thee? And there is nothing upon earth that I desire besides thee. My flesh and my heart may fail, but God is the strength of my heart and my portion for ever" (Psalm 73:24–26).

"Before I was afflicted I went astray; but now I keep thy word. It is good for me that I was afflicted, that I might learn thy statutes" (Psalm 119:67, 71).

"When he slew them, they sought for him; they repented and sought God earnestly. They remembered that God was their rock, and the Most High God their redeemer" (Psalm 78:34–35).

"In the world you have tribulation; but be of good cheer, I have overcome the world" (John 16:33).

Prayer:

Father of mercy and compassion, Helper of the helpless, look in tenderness upon the bereaved. Enable them to find Thy grace, strength and presence, thus to be sustained in this and all hours of life. Deliver them from all bitterness and despair by filling their desolate hearts with Thy forgiving love and Thy peace. Turn the shadows of death into the light of hope. Dispel lingering doubts with increased faith in the unseen world which is deeper than we have ever experienced, higher than we have ever known, more real than we have ever realized. Through Jesus Christ, our Lord, we pray. Amen.

Meditation:

NO TRAGEDIES TO THE CHRISTIAN

Our reaction to death is conditioned by the way in which it comes. If death comes at the end of a long, useful life, it comes as a welcomed guest, an answer to the oft-uttered sigh, "I have waited for thy salvation, O Lord." If death comes at the end of a lingering, agonizing illness, to a body cringed in pain, it comes as an angel of mercy. However, the visit of the death angel is not nearly so welcome when it comes in our midst with sudden and startling alarm. We are left stunned and bewildered.

In such an hour then, let us turn our anguished hearts for a message from Jesus, who says . . . "fear not them which kill the body, but are not able to kill the soul: but rather fear him which is able to destroy both soul and body in hell!" (Matthew 10:28, AV).

Physical death is no final disaster. This is the core of the Christian faith. Man is not primarily a body, rather he is a soul. This part of man cannot be kept alive on "bread alone," nor can it be killed by gunshot, knife blades, accident, flood, fire nor disease.

The body is but an earthly house for the dwelling of our souls. The house may become dilapidated and worn, or it may meet with calamity, but this does not mean defeat. "If our earthly house of this tabernacle were dissolved, we have a building of God, an house not made with hands, eternal in the heavens" (II Corinthians 5:1, AV). That has been the assurance of Christians throughout the centuries, vindicated by the resurrection of our Lord, Jesus Christ. This was the confidence which caused the Apostle Paul to write, "Who shall separate us from the love of Christ? Shall tribulation, or distress, or persecution, or famine, or nakedness, or peril, or sword? . . . No, in all these things we are more than conquerors through Him who loved us. For I am sure that neither death, nor life, nor angels, nor principalities, nor things present, nor things to come, nor powers, nor height, nor depth, nor anything else in all creation, will be able to separate us from the love of God in Christ Jesus our Lord" (Romans 8:35, 37–39).

What is a tragedy then? In the long perspective it is not a physical death nor an untimely accident, nor a malicious annihilation. Rather, tragedy is the spiritual death of the soul, living without contributing to the good of mankind, without taking the Kingdom of God seriously, without submitting to the Lordship of Christ. This is tragic for it kills the soul. Those experiences that burden the heart, make bitter the spirit, and depress the mind are enemies of the soul. A man's life does not consist in the things he possesses, nor in the abundance of his years, but in the quality of his soul. Let us not fear the forces that molest the body, rather let us guard our life from the enemies that disintegrate the soul. The wise prayer is not, "Lord, help me escape death and live a long life," but rather, "Lord, give me the spirit to live each day with a quality of eternity."

Benediction:

"Grace [be] to you and peace from God our Father and the Lord Jesus Christ" (I Corinthians 1:2).

Postlude:

"O God, Our Help in Ages Past"
"Abide with Me"
"Still, Still with Thee"

XII
For a Suicide Victim

Organ Prelude:

"Still, Still with Thee"
"Nearer, My God to Thee"
"I Need Thee Every Hour"

Opening Scriptural Sentence:

"Wait for the Lord; be strong, and let your heart take courage; yea, wait for the Lord! (Psalm 27:14). Thou dost keep him in perfect peace, whose mind is stayed on thee, because he trusts in thee" (Isaiah 23:6).

Invocation:

Almighty God, who art from everlasting to everlasting, a refuge and strength for those in trouble; lift our eyes beyond the scenes of earth, and grant us now the inward strength for this hour, in the name of Jesus Christ. Amen.

Hymn: (Optional) "My Faith Looks Up to Thee"

> My faith looks up to Thee,
>   Thou lamb of Calvary, Saviour divine!
> Now hear me while I pray,
>   Take all my guilt away,
> O let me from this day be wholly Thine.
>
> May Thy rich grace impart
>   Strength to my fainting heart, my zeal inspire;
> As Thou hast died for me,
>   O may my love to Thee,
> Pure, warm and changeless be, a living fire
>
> While life's dark maze I tread,
>   And griefs around me spread, be Thou my guide,
> Bid darkness turn to day;
>   Wipe sorrow's tears away,
> Nor let me ever stray from Thee aside.[1]

(Other appropriate hymn: "O, God, Our Help in Ages Past")

Scripture Reading:

"Have you not known? Have you not heard? The Lord is the everlasting God, the Creator of the ends of the earth. He does not faint or grow weary, his understanding is unsearchable. He gives power to the faint, and to him who has no might he increases strength. Even youths shall faint and be weary, and young men shall fall exhausted; but they who wait for the Lord shall renew their strength, they shall mount up with wings like eagles, they shall run and not be weary, they shall walk and not faint" (Isaiah 40:28–31).

". . . with everlasting love I will have compassion on you, says the Lord, your Redeemer. . . . For the mountains may depart and the hills be removed, but my steadfast love shall not depart from you, and my covenant of peace shall not be removed, says the Lord, who has compassion on you" (Isaiah 54:8, 10).

"I will not leave you desolate; I will come to you. . . . Peace I leave with you; my peace I give to you; not as the world gives do I give to you. Let not your hearts be troubled, neither let them be afraid" (John 14:18, 27).

Prayer:

O Father and God in heaven, in whose love is our hope, in whose wisdom is our life, in whose grace is our salvation, our confidence is in Thee.

In Thy infinite wisdom bring our imperfections to perfection, our marred works to completion, and in this midnight hour of life, bring the spirit of Thy comfort to us.

We offer Thee gratitude for the good traits of the one departed. We would fix our minds upon "whatever things were true, whatever things were honest, whatever things were just, whatever things were pure, whatever things were lovely, whatever things were of good report." Wherein there is virtue, we offer praise to Thee, O God.

For *his* dear ones, we pray deep faith, renewed confidence and courage to face this day and the tomorrows.

May we all experience the comradeship of Him who has carried our griefs and on whom the afflictions of us all have been laid. In this eternal fellowship keep us all until the morn eternal dawns and all the shadows have fled away and we see Thee face to face, through Jesus Christ, our Lord. Amen.

Hymn: (Optional) "Jesus, Lover of My Soul"

Jesus, Lover of my soul, Let me to Thy bosom fly,
While the nearer waters roll, While the tempest still is high;
Hide me, O my Saviour, hide, Till the storm of life is past;
Safe into the haven guide, O receive my soul at last.

Other refuge have I none, Hangs my helpless soul on Thee;
Leave, ah, leave me not alone, Still support and comfort me.
All my trust on Thee is stayed, All my help from Thee I bring;
Cover my defenseless head With the shadow of Thy wing.

Plenteous grace with Thee is found, Grace to cover all my sin;
Let the healing streams abound; Make and keep me pure within.
Thou of life the fountain art; Freely let me take of Thee;
Spring Thou up within my heart, Rise to all eternity.[2]

(Other appropriate hymn: "Lead, Kindly Light")

Meditation:

REST FROM THE BURDENS OF LIFE

Grief-smitten and deeply distressed, we have come to pay our closing tribute to a fellow comrade of the Way. May we be guided as well as comforted by the words of our Master who said, "Come to me, all who labour and are heavy-laden, and I will give you rest. Take my yoke upon you, and learn from me; for I am gentle and lowly in heart, and you will find rest for your souls. For my yoke is easy, and my burden is light" (Matthew 11:28–30). I ask two things of all of you.

I

First, that you think of this death as a rest from a troubled mind. Death is rest for those who are sick. It is release from the burdens and worries of life, escape from anguish and suffering. For many, the termination of the flesh is a welcome release—taking one to a state where the afflictions of body can bring no pain, and earthly toils can no longer weary, and the distress of troubled minds can be put to ease. Death is nature's merciful provision to terminate the flesh. Ah, it was this release for which Job begged, saying, "There the wicked cease from troubling, and there the weary are at rest" (Job 3:17).

While death is usually caused by physical accident or organic illness, this one has been caused by emotional sickness—deep, complex mental distress, confusion in outlook—sickness just as real as organic illness. For a spell, reason was dethroned; *he* lost control of *his* actions; *he* was driven helplessly to escape what evidently seemed to *him* an unbearable existence.

It is not our duty individually to condone or denounce, to pronounce judgment or censure, for that is committed to One who knows, the Lord our God. None of us has ever faced such a crisis of personality.

Sir Walter Scott said shortly before his death, "I feel as if I were to be myself again." The fast pace of this complex world does things to people's nerves, and minds. It certainly did so to this *man*. *He* was not *himself*. If *he* could take voice now, I am sure *he*, too, would say, "I feel as if I am myself again." *His* untimely death was an irresistible urge to find rest from something emotionally unbearable.

II

The second thing I want you to do is help eliminate the causes of this kind of breakdown. Our world can ill afford to lose capable citizens. We give some of our best energies and abilities to overcome disease and physical illness in order to prolong life. We should have the same aggressive concern to relieve the tensions and anxieties leading to this kind of illness.

Worry and fear take a terrific toll of lives in this modern age of strenuous living and excessive demands. War has slain its thousands, but worry is slaying its tens of thousands.

Many average and normal individuals like you and me have disturbed emotions, troubled minds, depressed and wounded spirits, unconscious evasions, fear and guilt complexes which are mountains in the way of wholesome living. A distinguished physician said, "The commonest and subtlest of all human diseases is fear."

There is only one prevention and one cure: that is faith—faith in God, faith in yourself, faith in your neighbors, faith in the ultimate triumph of righteousness, and faith in Christ who offers rest from the terrific pressures of life. "Come to me, all of you that are weary and heavy-laden, and I will give you rest." "Peace I leave with you; my peace I give to you; not as the world gives do I give to you" (John 14:27).

A newspaper editor told the story of a man who was born with a withered leg. From earliest infancy he had to wear a brace. As a boy, he could not run nor play nor climb trees with the other boys. Consequently, he developed a feeling of inferiority and fear until he not only had a brace on his leg but a brace on his mind. One day his father took him to the cathedral to pray for God to heal him. They knelt at the altar, beseeching God to heal the boy. Suddenly the boy cried out, "Father, Father, I have been healed." The boy leaped up—his leg was the same as before. But he had a different outlook, a new spirit, a radiant countenance. The boy said, "God has not taken the brace off my leg, but he has taken the brace off my mind."

Many of us have braces on our minds, but if you have

faith this mountain will remove, and the peace of God which passes all understanding shall guard your hearts. Trouble does not cease, but the worrying about it does. Pain is not remitted but the mental anguish is lost in peace. The burden is not removed, but another shoulder stoops to help share its load. Life becomes no easier, but it takes on new glory. Our responsibilities are not lightened, but the weariness of them is lost by having another help us bear them.

It is important to feel God's help and presence, to trust Him and to cast thy burdens upon the Lord.

The Lord is my light and my salvation; whom I shall fear?
The Lord is the strength of my life; of whom shall I be afraid?
Perfect love casteth out fear. If God be for us, who can be against us? I will trust and not be afraid. I will fear no evil, for Thou art with me.
O Love, that wilt not let me go, I rest my weary self in Thee;
I give Thee back the life I owe, that in Thine ocean depths its flow may richer, fuller be.

Benediction:

"The God of peace sanctify you wholly; your whole spirit and soul and body be preserved blameless unto the coming of our Lord Jesus Christ" (I Thessalonians 5:23, paraphrased).

Postlude:

"Abide with Me"
"O Jesus, I Have Promised"

XIII

For One Who Had Mental Illness

Prelude:

"Lead, Kindly Light"

Opening Scriptural Sentence:

"Trust in the Lord for ever, for the Lord God is an everlasting rock" (Isaiah 26:4).

Invocation:

"Eternal Spirit, in whom we live and move and have our being, in whom our life is thy joy, and death only an incident in the eternal adventure to which thou callest us; bring light out of the darkness, hope out of our sorrow, and comfort that rises out of an awareness of thy presence; we pray in the Spirit of Jesus. Amen."[1]

Scripture Reading:

"The eternal God is your dwelling place, and underneath are the everlasting arms" (Deuteronomy 33:27).

"Cast your burden on the Lord, and he will sustain you . . ." (Psalm 55:22).

"Are not two sparrows sold for a penny? And not one of them will fall to the ground without your Father's will. . . . Fear not, therefore; you are of more value than many sparrows" (Matthew 10:29, 31).

"Jesus said to her, 'I am the resurrection and the life; he who believes in me, though he die, yet shall he live, and whoever lives and believes in me shall never die . . .'" (John 11:25–26).

"He heals the brokenhearted, and binds up their wounds" (Psalm 147:3).

"Blessed are those who mourn, for they shall be comforted" (Matthew 5:4).

"There is therefore now no condemnation for those who are in Christ Jesus. . . . I consider that the sufferings of this present time are not worth comparing with the glory that is to be revealed to us. For the creation waits with eager longing for the revealing of the sons of God. . . . We know that in everything God works for good with those who love him, who are called according to his purpose. . . . What then shall we say to this? If God is for us, who is against us?" (Romans 8:1, 18–19, 28, 31).

Meditation:

THE PROMISES OF FAITH

The life of *him* who was friend and kinsman to those gathered here was precious to those who knew *him*. Even the handicap that was laid upon *him* did not make them cease to love *him*. So we have come in grateful remembrance to pay this tribute to *him* today.

We have come today to proclaim our faith that *his* life—*his* very being—was and is precious to our heavenly Father, our Creator, in an even greater measure than it is to us. "I am sure," wrote the Apostle, "that neither death, nor life, nor angels, nor principalities, nor things present, nor things to come, nor powers, nor height, nor depth, nor anything else in all creation, will be able to separate us from the love of God in Christ Jesus our Lord" (Romans 8:38–39).

This is the promise of our faith. "For we know that if the earthly tent we live in is destroyed, we have a building from God, a house not made with hands, eternal in the heavens. . . . For while we are still in this tent, we sigh with anxiety; not that we would be unclothed, but that we would be further clothed, so that what is mortal may be swallowed up by life" (II Corinthians 5:1, 4). We need not fear today, "For God hath not given us the spirit of fear; but of power, and of love, and of a sound mind" (II Timothy 1:7). *His* fears no longer plague *his* soul. They have been swallowed up in a new power and in greater love than we as yet have been given to know.

Among the papers of one who had suffered as *he* had suffered, and who at last found victory over her fears and uncertainties, were found these words, written out for her once by a Christian nurse or doctor, and repeated by her in her battle against fearfulness many times:

> For God is with me.
> He loves me.
> I can trust Him,
> So I will do my best.
> I won't be afraid.

This then, must be our faith and confidence at this time. "Yea, though I walk through the valley of the shadow of death, I will fear no evil: for thou art with me; thy rod and thy staff they comfort me" (Psalm 23:4, AV). "The eternal God is thy refuge, and underneath are the everlasting arms. . . ." (Deuteronomy 33:27).

> When the anxious hearts say, "Where?"
> God doth answer, "In my care."
> "Were they frightened at the last?"
> "No, the dread of death was past."
> "Do they need our tenderness?"
> "Where is love like mine to bless?"
> "Father, tell us where are they?"
> "In my keeping, night and day."[2]

Prayer:

Father of Mercies and God of all comfort, tenderly uphold these Thy children who feel most keenly this loss. They have drunk the cup of sorrow; wilt Thou now give them the cup of consolation. Give them the spirit of Him who learned obedience by the things which He suffered, so that like Him, they too may say in filial submission, "Not my will but thine be done." Comfort them with the assurance that their loved one is at rest in Thee; that all imperfections will be perfected; and that deeper than the pain and mystery of life and death are the everlasting arms of Thy tender mercy.

Benediction:

Now, may the God of all grace, who has called us into his eternal glory in Christ Jesus, . . . restore, establish and strengthen you. To him be glory and dominion for ever and ever. Amen.

Postlude:

"The Funeral March" (Chopin)
"Come, Sweet Repose" (Bach)

XIV

For a Person of Poor Reputation

Prelude:

"There's a Wideness in God's Mercy" (Emmelar)
"My Heart Is Filled with Longing" (Bach)
"My Faith Looks Up to Thee"

Opening Scriptural Sentence:

"For as the heavens are high above the earth, so great is his steadfast love toward those who fear him. . . . As a father pities his children, so the Lord pities those who fear him. For he knows our frame; he remembers that we are dust" (Psalm 103:11, 13–14).

Invocation:

Almighty God, unto whom all hearts are open, all desires known, and from whom no secrets are hid: cleanse the thoughts of our minds by the inspiration of Thy Holy Spirit, that we may perfectly love Thee and worthily magnify Thy Holy Name, through Jesus Christ our Lord. Amen.

Hymn: (Optional) "Come, Ye Disconsolate"

(This may be organ music, choral anthem, vocal solo, or spoken)

> Come, ye disconsolate, where'er ye languish,
> Come to the mercy-seat, fervently kneel;
> Here bring your wounded hearts, here tell your
>   anguish;
> Earth has no sorrow that heaven cannot heal.
>
> Joy of the desolate, light of the straying,
> Hope of the penitent, fadeless and pure!
> Here speaks the Comforter, tenderly saying,
> "Earth has no sorrow that heaven cannot cure."
>
> Here see the Bread of Life; see waters flowing
> Forth from the throne of God, pure from above:
> Come to the feast prepared; come, ever knowing,
> Earth has no sorrow but heaven can remove.[1]

(Other appropriate hymn: "There Is a Balm in Gilead")

Scripture Reading:

"O Lord, thou hast searched me and known me! Thou knowest when I sit down and when I rise up; thou discernest my thoughts from afar. Thou searchest out my path and my lying down, and art acquainted with all my ways. Even before a word is on my tongue, lo, O Lord, thou knowest it altogether. Thou dost beset me behind and before, and layest thy hand upon me. Such knowledge is too wonderful for me; it is high, I cannot attain it. Whither shall I go from thy Spirit? Or whither shall I flee from thy presence? If I ascend to heaven, thou art there! If I make my bed in Sheol, thou art there! If I take the wings of the morning and dwell in the uttermost parts of the sea, even there thy hand shall lead me, and thy right hand shall hold me" (Psalm 139:1–10).

"Beloved, let us love one another; for love is of God, and he who loves is born of God and knows God. He who does not love does not know God; for God is love. In this the love of God was made manifest among us, that God sent his only Son into the world, so that we might live through him. In this is love, not that we loved God but that he loved us and sent his Son to be the expiation for our sins. Beloved, if God so loved us, we also ought to love one another. No man has ever seen God; if we love one another, God abides in us and his love is perfected in us. By this we know that we abide in him and he in us, because he has given us of his own Spirit. And we have seen and testify that the Father has sent his Son as the Savior of the world. Whoever confesses that Jesus is the Son of God, God abides in him, and he in God. So we know and believe the love God has for us. God is love, and he who abides in love abides in God, and God abides in him. In this is love perfected with us, that we may have confidence for the day of judgment, because as he is so are we in this world. There is no fear in love, but perfect love casts out fear. For fear has to do with punishment, and he who fears is not perfected in love. We love, because he first loved us. If any one says, 'I love God,' and hates his brother, he is a liar; for he who does not love his brother whom he has seen, cannot love God whom he has not seen. And this commandment we have from him, that he who loves God should love his brother also" (I John 4:7–21).

Prayer:

O Lover of our souls; whose mercy is everlasting, and whose understanding knows no limits: we turn to Thee. Cause us to know how utterly we are in Thy care, how entirely we are bounded by Thee on every side, how completely we are cast on Thy mercy. Known to Thee are all our failings, our needs, our sorrows and griefs. Without Thee, we are poor and weak; with Thee we can be brave and strong.

Thou dost gird and guide us, though often we know it not. The shadow with which Thou darkenest our way, is but the shadow of Thy close approaching and overbrooding presence. In death and in life, in sorrow as in joy, Thou art waiting to bless with love and forgiveness, if we but turn to Thee—in the name of Christ, the Saviour, Amen.

Solo: (Optional) "God So Loved the World"

> God so loved the world, that He gave His only Son,
> That whoso believeth, should not perish,
>   but have everlasting life.
> For God sent not His Son into the world to condemn
>   the world,
> But that the world through Him might be saved.[2]

(Other appropriate solos: "The Love of God," "Love Divine")

Meditation:

GOD'S BOUNDLESS LOVE

Death forces us to trust the Almighty. At death we come to the end of human knowledge, human power, and human comfort. We are left to the mercy of God. Comforting it is, therefore, to have a God to trust of perfect love, absolute knowledge, boundless forgiveness, and infinite patience. "God is love" is a glorious fact to lean upon.

John Greenleaf Whittier, the famous Quaker poet, beautifully shared his faith with all posterity through his poetry. The key to his life's philosophy, and the quality which gives his work permanence, was his emphasis upon the unfathomable love of God. In none of his poetry is it more profoundly related than in his "Eternal Goodness":

Yet, in the maddening maze of things,
   And tossed by storm and flood,
To one fixed trust my spirit clings;
   I know that God is good!

*   *   *

I long for household voices gone
   For vanished smiles I long,
But God hath led my dear ones on,
   And He can do no wrong.

I know not what the future hath
   Of marvel or surprise,
Assured alone that life and death
   His mercy underlies.

*   *   *

And so beside the Silent Sea
   I wait with muffled oar;
No harm from Him can come to me
   On ocean or on shore.

> I know not where His islands lift
>   Their fronded palms in air;
> I only know I cannot drift
>   Beyond His love and care.[3]

So today, for comfort and hope, let us turn our thoughts
to the love of God. He cares for us even when we do not
deserve it. God believes the best about us; He sees the beautiful, the potential, the hidden qualities of the spirit. How often we are judgmental, looking for weaknesses, believing the
worst even with partial knowledge. Paul, the Apostle who
wrote the great Hymn of Love, also said, "Whatever is true,
whatever is honorable, whatever is just, whatever is pure,
whatever is lovely, whatever is gracious, if there is any excellence, if there is anything worthy of praise, think about
these things." Jesus our Saviour, said, "Judge not that you
be not judged. For with the judgment you pronounce you
will be judged, and the measure you give will be the measure
you get." When Jesus faced what He knew was certain
death, He said, "I am not alone, because the Father is with
me." Jesus is saying now to those who are grieved and bewildered, "You are not alone for the Heavenly Father is
with you." What a difference that assurance made to Jesus
in dark Gethsemane, and what a difference it can make to
you. With the psalmist we can say, "Whither shall I go
from thy Spirit? Or whither shall I flee from thy presence?
If I ascend to heaven, thou art there! If I make my bed in
Sheol, thou art there! If I take the wings of the morning, and
dwell in the uttermost parts of the sea, even there thy hand
shall lead me, and thy right hand shall hold me." "Let not
your hearts be troubled," said the Master, "believe in God,
believe also in me."

If there were no God, we might despair today. If there
were no "Jesus-like God," there would be nothing to give

consolation or strength or hope for such an hour. If there were no complete understanding at the heart of the universe, the pronouncement of judgment would be ours; nevertheless, because of God, before whom pass the generations of men, the prerogative of judgment is His alone—and "God is love." Shall not the Judge of all the earth do right? Will He not be considerate? Let not your hearts be baffled, troubled, distressed beyond comfort. This is God's sorrow even more than it is your sorrow. We need not fear if we trust God. God is a God of sympathy, understanding, and love.

This is the truth upon which we depend in life's last crisis. If there is a God such as Jesus revealed, and there has to be some Ultimate Reality from which the Spirit of Jesus came, then we can meet any emergency with fearless confidence.

Benediction:

O Christ, make us instruments of Thy peace. Where there is hatred, let us sow love; where there is injury, pardon; where there is discord, union; where there is doubt, faith; where there is despair, hope; where there is darkness, light; where there is sadness, joy. Grant that we may not so much seek to be consoled, as to console; to be understood as to understand; to be loved as to love; for it is in giving that we receive, it is in pardoning that we are pardoned; and it is in dying that we are born to eternal life. Through Jesus Christ, our Lord. Amen.[4]

Postlude:

"Faith" (Mendelssohn)
"Nearer, My God, to Thee"

XV

For an Older Mother

Prelude Music:

"Now the Day Is Over"

"My Faith Looks Up to Thee"

Opening Scriptural Sentence:

"He who dwells in the shelter of the Most High, who abides in the shadow of the Almighty, will say to the Lord, 'My refuge and my fortress; my God, in whom I trust' " (Psalm 91:1–2).

Invocation:

Almighty God, our Heavenly Father, who art our refuge and strength, a very present help in time of trouble; enable us, we pray Thee, to put our trust in Thee, and seeing that we have an High Priest who is touched with the feeling of our infirmities, may we come unto the throne of grace that we may obtain mercy and find grace to help in this our time of need; through Jesus Christ our Lord. Amen.

Scripture Reading:

"Bless the Lord, O my soul; and all that is within me, bless his holy name! Bless the Lord, O my soul, and forget not all his benefits" (Psalm 103:1–2).

"A good wife who can find? She is far more precious than jewels. The heart of her husband trusts in her, and he will have no lack of gain. She does him good, and not harm, all the days of her life. . . . She opens her hand to the poor, and reaches out her hands to the needy. . . . Strength and dignity are her clothing, and she laughs at the time to come. She opens her mouth with wisdom, and the teaching of kindness is on her tongue. She looks well to the ways of her household, and does not eat the bread of idleness. Her children rise up and call her blessed; her husband also, and he praises her: 'Many women have done excellently, but you surpass them all.' Charm is deceitful, and beauty is vain, but a woman who fears the Lord is to be praised. Give her of the fruit of her hands, and let her works praise her in the gates" (Proverbs 31:10–12, 20, 25–31).

"Jesus said to her, 'I am the resurrection and the life; he who believes in me, though he die, yet shall he live, and whoever lives and believes in me shall never die. Do you believe this?' " (John 11:25–26).

"Let not your hearts be troubled; believe in God, believe also in me. In my Father's house are many rooms; if it were not so, would I have told you that I go to prepare a place for you? And when I go and prepare a place for you, I will come again and will take you to myself, that where I am you may be also" (John 14:1–3).

Prayer:

O Thou, who art the strength of those who suffer, the repose of the weary, and the provider for the deceased: we thank Thee for the boundless blessings that attend our earthly pathways—especially for the life of the one we honor. For her character, the breadth of her sympathies, the patience of her understanding, the calmness of her spirit even in anguish and distress, we acknowledge in gratitude before Thee, from whom come all things good. We thank Thee for her courage, her knowledge of Thee, her devotion to Christ and His church, and her good family. We commend her to Thee, O God, for shelter in the promised inheritance that is incorruptible, undefiled, and that fadeth not away. We beseech Thee, merciful Lord, to bless with the bonds of Christian love the family circle that is severed. Help us all to be more resolute in our Christian devotion, as we wait for the cloudless day to dawn when earthly shadows shall flee away and death shall be no more—through Jesus Christ, our Lord, Amen.

Hymn: (Optional) "O Love That Wilt Not Let Me Go"

(This may be organ music, choral anthem, vocal solo, or spoken)

O Love, that wilt not let me go,
   I rest my weary soul in Thee;
I give Thee back the life I owe,
That in Thine ocean depths its flow
   May richer, fuller be.

O Light, that followest all my way,
   I yield my flickering torch to Thee;
My heart restores its borrowed ray,
That in Thy sunshine's blaze its day
   May brighter, fairer be.

O Joy, that seekest me through pain,
   I cannot close my heart to Thee;
I trace the rainbow through the rain,
And feel the promise is not vain,
   That morn shall tearless be.

O Cross, that liftest up my head,
   I dare not ask to fly from Thee;
I lay in dust, life's glory dead,
And from the ground there blossoms red
   Life that shall endless be.[1]

Meditation:

THE AFTERGLOW OF A MOTHER'S LIFE

This is a tender hour, but in no wise an hour of tragedy. There is something utterly appropriate about the going of one who has lived a long, happy, and useful life, who has given so much of love, kindness to her family, community, her friends, and her church. This is not a time of darkness, but a time of light, not of exaggerated grief but of gratitude to God for this life that *was, and is, and shall continue to be.* Today, we shall not talk about death, but of life.

The most beautiful part of day comes in the cool of the evening. The other night we were awed with the beautiful splendor of the sunset. It had been a hot, sultry day. Time moved so slowly. As night approached, a peaceful silence came across the face of the earth, waiting for the pageantry of the night. Slowly the sun went down, finally out of sight. What cool peace. What wonderful release. But there, for one magnificent moment, was the startling beauty of the day's afterglow. Indescribable colors, created by the sun's rays reflecting back upon the clouds, covered the entire western sky.

Just so, today we see the afterglow of a beautiful life.

Proverbs 10:7 records, "The memory of the just is blessed." Henrik Ibsen, the Norwegian author, in his book *The House of Rosmersholm* tells of a rector who is danger- ously tempted to do evil, but each time he is at the point of yielding, he looks at the portraits of his godly ancestors which hang on the wall of his home. Each speaks a word holding him back.

Harriet Beecher Stowe, the author of *Uncle Tom's Cabin*, used to say it was her brother's recollection of their mother and their hope of meeting her in heaven, that held them back from many a temptation and sin. There is a saving and guarding power in the memory of a godly mother who has gone before us. "The memory of the just is blessed."

Well it is, then, to gaze in this final tribute, upon the afterglow of this mother's life.

Temple Bailey has written a parable on motherhood:

The young mother set her foot on the path of life. "Is the way long?" she asked. And her guide said, "Yes, and the way is hard. And you will be old before you reach the end of it. But the end will be better than the beginning." But the young mother was happy and she would not believe that anything could be better than these years. So she played with her children and gathered flowers for them along the way and bathed with them in the clear streams; and the sun shone on them and life was good, and the young mother cried, "Nothing will ever be lovelier than this."

Then night came, and storm, and the path was dark and the children shook with fear and cold, and the mother drew them close and covered them with her mantle and the children said, "O mother, we are not afraid, for you are near, and no harm can come," and the mother said, "This is better than the brightness of day, for I have taught my children courage."

And the morning came, and there was a hill ahead and the children climbed and grew weary, and the mother was weary, but at all times she said to the children, "A little patience and we are there." So the children climbed and when they reached the top, they said, "We could not have done it without you, mother." And the mother, when she lay down that night, looked up at the stars and said, "This is a better day than the last, for my children have learned fortitude in the face of hardness. Yesterday I gave them courage, today I have given them strength."

And the next day came strange clouds which darkened the earth—clouds of war and hate and evil—and the children groped and stumbled and the mother said, "Look up. Lift your eyes to the light." And the children looked and saw above the clouds an Everlasting Glory, and it guided them and brought them beyond the darkness. And that night the mother said, "This is the best day of all, for I have shown my children God."

And the days went on, and the weeks and the months and the years, and the mother grew old, and she was little and bent. But her children were tall and strong and walked with courage. And when the way was rough they lifted her, for she was as light as a feather; and at last they came to a hill, and beyond the hill they could see a shining road and golden gates flung wide.

And the mother said, "I have reached the end of my journey. And now I know that the end is better than the beginning, for my children can walk alone, and their children after them."

And the children said, "You will always walk with us, Mother, even when you have gone through the gates."

And they stood and watched her as she went on alone, and the gates closed after her. And they said, "We cannot see her, but she is with us still. A mother like ours is more than a memory. She is a Living Presence."[2]

Benediction:

"And the peace of God, which passes all understanding, will keep your hearts and your minds in Christ Jesus" (Philippians 4:7).

Postlude:

"Now the Day Is Over"
"Sunset and Evening Star"
"Hark, Hark, My Soul"
"Going Home"

XVI

For an Aged Father

Prelude:

"Near to the Heart of God"
"Largo" (Handel)

Opening Scriptural Sentence:

"Who shall ascend the hill of the Lord? And who shall stand in his holy place? He who has clean hands and a pure heart, who does not lift up his soul to what is false, and does not swear deceitfully. He will receive blessing from the Lord, and vindication from the God of his salvation" (Psalm 24:3–5).

Invocation:

O God, who revealed Thy love to us in Jesus Christ, in this hour it comforts us to know that the friendship of our souls with Thee is eternal, and that nothing in life and death is able to separate us from Thee. Committed to Thy fatherly care, we face the future with calm confidence and inward joy—through Jesus Christ our Lord. Amen.

Hymn: (Optional) "From All That Dwell Below the Skies"

(To be sung by congregation)

> From all that dwell below the skies
> Let the Creator's praise arise;
> Let the Redeemer's Name be sung
> Through every land, by every tongue.
> Eternal are Thy mercies, Lord;

Eternal truth attends Thy word:
Thy praise shall sound from shore to shore
Till suns shall rise and set no more. Amen.[1]

Scripture Reading:

"Lord, thou hast been our dwelling place in all generations. Before the mountains were brought forth, or ever thou
hadst formed the earth and the world, from everlasting to
everlasting thou art God. Thou turnest man back to the dust
and sayest, 'Turn back, O children of men!' For a thousand
years in thy sight are but as yesterday when it is past, or as a
watch in the night. . . . The years of our life are threescore
and ten, or even by reason of strength fourscore; yet their
span is but toil and trouble; they are soon gone, and we fly
away. . . . So teach us to number our days that we may
get a heart of wisdom. . . . Satisfy us in the morning with
thy steadfast love, that we may rejoice and be glad all our
days. Make us glad as many days as thou hast afflicted us,
and as many years as we have seen evil. Let thy work be
manifest to thy servants, and thy glorious power to their
children. Let the favor of the Lord our God be upon us, and
establish thou the work of our hands upon us, yea, the work
of our hands establish thou it" (Psalm 90:1-4, 10. 12, 14-
17).

"We know that if our earthly house of this tabernacle
were dissolved, we have a building of God, an house not
made with hands, eternal in the heavens" (II Corinthians
5:1 AV).

"After this I looked, and behold, a great multitude which
no man could number, from every nation, from all tribes
and peoples and tongues, standing before the throne and
before the Lamb, clothed in white robes, with palm branches
in their hands, and crying out with a loud voice, 'Salvation

belongs to our God who sits upon the throne, and to the Lamb.' And all the angels stood round the throne and round the elders and the four living creatures, and they fell on their faces before the throne and worshiped God, saying, 'Amen! Blessing and glory and wisdom and thanksgiving and honor and power and might be to our God for ever and ever! Amen.' Then one of the elders addressed me, saying, 'Who are these, clothed in white robes, and whence have they come?' I said to him, 'Sir, you know.' And he said to me, 'These are they who have come out of the great tribulation; they have washed their robes and made them white in the blood of the Lamb. Therefore are they before the throne of God, and serve him day and night in his temple; and he who sits upon the throne will shelter them with his presence. They shall hunger no more, neither thirst any more; the sun shall not strike them, nor any scorching heat. For the Lamb in the midst of the throne will be their shepherd, and he will guide them to springs of living water; and God will wipe away every tear from their eyes' " (Revelation 7:9–17).

Prayer:

Our Father in Heaven, we are grateful we have a Father of our souls, who dost listen and answer each simple and sincere prayer, and who art loving, approachable and compassionate.

We thank Thee for the life of this earthly father who has been called away from this existence. We are grateful for his many years upon earth, for the many things in his fatherly character which endeared him to his family and friends. We are grateful for his good qualities which commend him to Thy keeping, and which give assurance that he knows heights where he now is which can never fully be known on earth. Having fought the good fight, having finished his course, and having kept the faith, wilt Thou grant unto him the crown of life that fadeth not away.

May the family which he leaves behind be comforted and strengthened by Thine everlasting arms. Help them to know that deeper than the pain and mystery of death is Thy tender love and mercy. And may they exemplify the good qualities of this father, and the Saviour Jesus Christ, in whom there is life abundant and eternal. Amen.

Meditation:

KEEPING FAITH

The words which seem appropriate today are those of a Christian veteran who said, as he came to the close of life, "I have fought a good fight"—he had been involved in the struggle against the enemies of mankind; "I have finished my course"—he had made the most of life, leaving the world richer because of his living; "I have kept the faith." The Apostle Paul had kept something even as he moved hither and yon throughout the Mediterranean world.

People today are on the move. They are moving geographically here and there. People change physically, with every cell in one's body changing every seven years. Socially and spiritually one does not stand still. In this constant change, one vital question should be faced, "What are you keeping?"

Like the Apostle Paul, the one in whose memory we are met kept the faith.

I

He kept faith with his wife. When two people enter the marriage bond, they do so as an adventure of faith. Neither one knows that the other will always be attractive or cooperative. They accept each other on faith, taking their vows, "for better, for worse, for richer, for poorer." Faith is a lovely thing at the marriage altar, but it is far more lovely after many, many wedding anniversaries have been celebrated at which one can say, "Now abideth faith, hope, love —but the greatest of these is love." This man kept faith with his wife.

II

Furthermore, he kept faith with his children. When parents bring children into the world, that too, is an adventure of faith. They cannot be sure the child will be normal, mentally or physically; they just venture on faith. They do not know whether the child will bring honor or shame to the family; they proceed with faith. On the other hand, the children cannot know whether the parents will keep faith with them. They may disappoint them, or forsake them. The poet Gillilan said of his father:

> He was my own until I fully knew
> And never could forget how deep and true
> A father's love for his own son may be.
> It drew me nearer God Himself; for He
> Has loved His son. These are but grateful tears
> That he was with me all those happy years.[2]

Rufus Jones, the late Quaker teacher and writer, lost an only son at the age of eleven years. But the boy continued for forty-five years to be a dominant influence in his father's life. The Jones study at Haverford contained many photographs of distinguished personalities, but in the center of the mantel was the portrait of the boy, Lowell. Rufus Jones felt he had to live for that son. Writing forty years after the lad's death, he said, "I overheard him once talking with a group of playmates, when each was telling what he wanted to be when he grew up, and Lowell said, when his turn came, 'I want to grow up and be a man like my daddy.' Few things in my life have given me greater impulse to dedication. What kind of a man was I going to be, if I was to be the pattern for my boy?"[3] Rufus Jones never lost faith with that boy.

III

Again, this man kept faith with his friends. An unknown poet has written:

> My greatest joy on earth shall be,
> To find at the turning of every road,
> The strong hand of a comrade kind,
> To help me onward with my load.
>
> But since I have no gold to give
> And only love can make amends,
> My daily prayer in life shall be,
> "God make me worthy of my friends."

IV

Then, most important of all, he kept faith in God. He started early in life with faith in God, and he kept that faith to the end. It was the realization that a greater power was behind his life that gave him courage, that kept a song in his heart, light in his eyes, and made him expendable for the Kingdom of God. He had faith that God had destined him to live beyond the earth, and that there was laid up for him, and for all those who love the Lord, a crown of righteousness. That was the conviction that kept him going.

In II Kings 2:9 one can read the interesting conversation of Elijah, shortly before his departure from the earth, with his young son in the faith, Elisha. The elderly prophet says, "Ask what I shall do for you, before I am taken from you." The young man with insight, high ideals, and profound ap-

preciation, responded, asking not for worldly inheritance,
nor fame and honor, but rather, "I pray you, let me inherit a
double portion of your spirit." How fitting a request for a
son to ask, of a worthy father.

Solo: (Optional) "Wonderful Peace"

> Far away in the depths of my spirit tonight
> Rolls a melody sweeter than psalm;
> In celestial like strains it unceasingly falls,
> O'er my soul like an infinite calm.
>
> *Chorus:*
> Peace, peace, wonderful peace,
> Coming down from the Father above;
> Sweep over my spirit for ever, I pray;
> In fathomless billows of love.
>
> What a treasure I have in this wonderful peace,
> Buried deep in the heart of my soul,
> So secure that no power can mine it away,
> While the years of eternity roll!
>
> And methinks when I rise to that city of peace,
> Where the Author of peace I shall see,
> That one strain of the song which the ransomed will
>   sing
> In that heavenly kingdom shall be:[4]

Benediction:

   "Grace to you and peace from God our Father and the
Lord Jesus Christ" (I Corinthians I:3).

Postlude:

   "Largo" ("Going Home," Dvorak)
   "Now the Day Is Over"
   "Sunset and Evening Star"

XVII

For a Stranger

Prelude:

"Consolation," Mendelssohn
"Oh, Rest in the Lord," Mendelssohn
"I Need Thee Every Hour"

Opening Scriptural Sentence:

"Have you not known? Have you not heard? The Lord is the everlasting God, the Creator of the ends of the earth. He does not faint or grow weary, his understanding is unsearchable. He gives power to the faint, and to him who has no might he increases strength" (Isaiah 40:28–29).

Invocation:

Our Father and our God, who art from everlasting to everlasting, before whose face pass all generations of men: we bow reverently before Thee. In Thy understanding are all our ways, in Thy love is our hope, and in Thy wisdom is our future. Grant us now, confidence and trust in Thy tender mercies and fatherly care, through Jesus Christ, our Lord. Amen.

Hymn: (Optional) "I Know Not What the Future Hath"
(This may be organ music, choral anthem, vocal solo, or spoken)

> I know not what the future hath
> Of marvel or surprise,
> Assured alone that life and death
> His mercy underlies.

And if my heart and flesh are weak
To bear an untried pain,
The bruisèd reed He will not break,
But strengthen and sustain.

And Thou, O Lord, by whom are seen
Thy creatures as they be,
Forgive me if too close I lean
My human heart on Thee!

And so beside the Silent Sea
I wait with muffled oar;
No harm from Him can come to me
On ocean or on shore.

I know not where His islands lift
Their fronded palms in air;
I only know I cannot drift
Beyond His love and care.[1]

Scripture Reading:

"Lord, let me know my end, and what is the measure of my days; let me know how fleeting my life is! Behold, thou hast made my days a few handbreadths, and my lifetime is as nothing in thy sight. Surely every man stands as a mere breath! Surely man goes about as a shadow! Surely for nought are they in turmoil; man heaps up, and knows not who will gather! And now, Lord, for what do I wait? My hope is in thee. Deliver me from all my transgressions. Make me not the scorn of the fool! I am dumb, I do not open my mouth; for it is thou who has done it. Remove thy stroke from me; I am spent by the blows of thy hand. When thou dost chasten man with rebukes for sin, thou dost consume like a moth what is dear to him; surely every man is a mere breath! Hear my prayer, O Lord, and give ear to my cry; hold not thy peace at my tears! For I am thy passing guest, a sojourner, like all my fathers. Look away from me, that I may know gladness, before I depart and be no more!" (Psalm 39:4–13).

"Do not lay up for yourselves treasures on earth, where moth and rust consume and where thieves break in and steal, but lay up for yourselves treasures in heaven, where neither moth nor rust consumes and where thieves do not break in and steal. For where your treasure is, there will your heart be also. . . . But seek first his kingdom and his righteousness, and all these things shall be yours as well" (Matthew 6:19–21, 33).

"Every one then who hears these words of mine and does them will be like a wise man who built his house upon the rock; and the rain fell, and the floods came, and the winds blew and beat upon that house, but it did not fall, because it had been founded upon the rock. And every one who hears these words of mine and does not do them will be like a foolish man who built his house upon the sand; and the rain fell, and the floods came, and the winds blew and beat against that house, and it fell; and great was the fall of it" (Matthew 7:24–27).

Meditation:

FACING DEATH VICTORIOUSLY

On this occasion when we meet to pay tribute to our loved one, it is not our purpose to eulogize, though many commendable things could well be said as you who are here well know. Nor is it our purpose to pronounce any ecclesiastical judgment for such is the prerogative of the Eternal God, who alone shall determine the destinies of us all according to our life on earth. It is, rather, my purpose today to speak words of comfort and faith to you who mourn this passing.

All of us need to learn how to live as if we would die tonight, and to work as if we would live forever. For not until we look at death victoriously can we learn to live victoriously; and not until we live victoriously can we face death victoriously.

Therefore, let us look to Jesus, the Master and Lord of life, who teaches us four lessons in facing death.

I

First, Jesus teaches us not to fear those who can destroy the body only. "Rather," said He, "fear him who can destroy both the soul and the body in hell." Jesus taught that to assume the physical part of life as the primary part can only lead to defeat, for it is written, "Man shall not live by bread alone, but by every word of God." When we assume that the body is ultimate, all our values are reversed in life.

Man is primarily a soul—his spirit is his real self. That is what makes him distinctive, different from mere organic animals; this is the mark of divine sonship. These bodies are mere houses for our spirits, physical equipment which has been granted for our temporary expression. What happens to us externally is important only so far as it has inner results.

When one is not afraid of the influences which threaten the body, then he does not despair in melancholy when the physical body is outworn or destroyed by accident, or hampered by disease. When one realizes that death is no final disaster, he too can face suffering with confidence as did Jesus. He too can say, as did John Quincy Adams, when asked how he was, "John Quincy Adams is very well, sir, very well. The house in which he has been living so many years is dilapidated and old. He has received word from the owner that he must vacate soon—but John Quincy Adams is very well, thank you."[2]

II

Jesus teaches us, also, that there are some things worse than dying. In fact, there are many things worse than dying. This sounds like a revolutionary doctrine, for most of us assume death to be the worst thing that could happen to any family or any person. We are always reluctant for death to enter our circle of friends, and that is quite natural. This world is filled with people, who in the deepest recesses of their hearts, would gladly trade their worldly success for a clear conscience, peace of mind, and a Christian character. The loss of virtue, sacrificing human beings for selfish benefits, denying truth for the sake of a lie, failing to do our rightful duty—these things are far worse than dying, for killing the soul is the eternal death. These kill the quality of soul, and when a man loses his soul, he loses everything.

III

Jesus teaches us, furthermore, that the quality of life is more important than the length of life. Science has learned how to preserve and lengthen man's life. Indeed, man's average length of years has been increased from forty-five to sixty-five, and promises to go beyond that. Modern medicine can cure our bodies of nearly every malady. It is marvelous. We take pride in long life, but what if we have nothing to live for? There is no virtue in number of years, if we have not learned how to live. Quality is more important than quantity. Sometimes we actually live more in one day than we do in months, or more in one hour than we do in an entire day. We sometimes hear the remark, "What a tragic death" —and we usually mean the death of a child or youth who passes prematurely. However, the most tragic death is that of the one who has never really learned to live. When a man dies without friends—that is tragic. When a person dies

without ever having contributed to the good of the world—
that is disaster. When a person dies without having created
within a spirit worthy of fellowship with God—that is ultimate failure. A man's life consisteth not in the things he
possesses nor in the abundance of his years, but in the quality of his living. The primary question is not "When shall
death come to me?" but this, "How shall I live to please
God?"

> For when the One Great Scorer comes
> To write against your name,
> He writes—not that you won or lost—
> But how you played the game.[3]

IV

*Finally, Jesus teaches by demonstration that human life
exists beyond the grave, and death is the doorway to the
future.* Edwin Arlington Robinson closed his dramatic dia-
logue with this conviction when he said, "I shall have more
to say when I am dead."

Benjamin Franklin, who died in 1790, wrote this epitaph
for his monument:

> The Body of
> Franklin Printer,
> (Like the Cover of an old Book
> Its Contents torn out
> And stript of its Lettering and Gilding)
> Lies here, Food for Worms,
> But the Work shall not be lost;
> For it will, (as he believ'd) appear once more,
> In a new and more elegant Edition
> Revised and corrected,
> By the Author.

This is our faith! Without the experience of death, we could never know the future. And we can never know the beautiful future without experiencing Jesus Christ who said, "Because I live, you shall also live . . . 'He who believes in me, though he die, yet shall he live, and whoever lives and believes in me shall never die. Do you believe this?' " (John 11:25–26).

Prayer:

Heavenly Father, whose Son Jesus wept at the grave of His friend Lazarus, look, we pray Thee, with compassion upon those now in sorrow and affliction. We come to Thee because of our need of Thy love and understanding. Without Thee we are poor and weak; with Thee we can be brave and strong. Grant us sure confidence in Thy care and blessings which Thou art more willing to give than we are to receive.

We ask the benediction of Thy presence upon the one who passed to the unknown future. Thou knowest the frailties and weaknesses; Thou knowest too the aspirations and hopes. Let us not enter into judgment upon the other. Rather, bestow new opportunities of service and encouragement to growth so that both *he* and we may grow more and more in Thy fullness.

Benediction:

"To the King of ages, immortal, invisible, the only God, be honor and glory for ever and ever. Amen" (I Timothy 1:17).

Postlude:
  "Resignation" (Mendelssohn)
  "O Mother Dear, Jerusalem" (Samuel A. Ward)
  "Abide with Me"

XVIII
For an Outstanding Christian

Prelude:

"Largo" (Dvorak)
"Ten Thousand Times Ten Thousand"

Opening Scriptural Sentence:

"Jesus said to her, 'I am the resurrection and the life; he who believes in me, though he die, yet shall he live, and whoever lives and believes in me shall never die . . .'" (John 11:25–26).

Invocation:

O God, the Lord of life, the Conqueror over death, the Repose of the faithful, our help in every time of trouble: to Thee we lift our thoughts and voices in adoration and praise, in the name of Jesus Christ, who taught us how to pray saying: (Unison)

Our Father who art in heaven,
Hallowed be thy name.
Thy kingdom come,
Thy will be done,
On earth as it is in heaven.
Give us this day our daily bread;
And forgive us our debts,
As we also have forgiven our debtors;
And lead us not into temptation,
But deliver us from evil.
For thine is the kingdom, and the power.
And the glory, forever. Amen.

"Gloria Patri" (Congregation)

Hymn: (Optional) "Blessed Assurance"

(This may be sung by congregation, or as a solo)

> Blessed assurance, Jesus is mine!
> O what a foretaste of glory, divine!
> Heir of salvation, purchased of God,
> Born of His spirit, washed in His blood.
>
> *Chorus:*
> This is my story, this is my song,
> Praising my Saviour, all the day long;
> This is my story, this is my song,
> Praising my Saviour all the day long.
>
> Perfect submission, perfect delight,
> Visions of rapture now burst on my sight.
> Angels descending, bring from above
> Echoes of mercy, whispers of love.
>
> Perfect submission, all is at rest,
> I in my Saviour am happy and blest,
> Watching and waiting, looking above,
> Filled with His goodness, lost in His love.[1]

Scripture Reading:

"The Lord is my shepherd, I shall not want; he makes m
lie down in green pastures. He leads me beside still wate
he restores my soul. He leads me in paths of righteousne
for his name's sake. Even though I walk through the vall
of the shadow of death, I fear no evil; for thou art w
me; thy rod and thy staff, they comfort me. Thou prepar
a table before me in the presence of my enemies; th
anointest my head with oil, my cup overflows. Surely goo
ness and mercy shall follow me all the days of my life; a
I shall dwell in the house of the Lord for ever" (Psalm 2.

"Let not your hearts be troubled; believe in God, believe also in me. In my Father's house are many rooms; if it were not so, would I have told you that I go to prepare a place for you? And when I go and prepare a place for you, I will come again and will take you to myself, that where I am you may be also" (John 14:1–3).

"For this perishable nature must put on the imperishable, and this mortal nature must put on immortality. When the perishable puts on the imperishable, and the mortal puts on immortality, then shall come to pass the saying that is written: 'Death is swallowed up in victory.' 'O death, where is thy victory? O death, where is thy sting?' The sting of death is sin, and the power of sin is the law. But thanks be to God, who gives us the victory through our Lord Jesus Christ. Therefore, my beloved brethren, be steadfast, immovable, always abounding in the work of the Lord, knowing that in the Lord your labor is not in vain" (I Corinthians 15:53–58).

"Bless the Lord, O my soul, and forget not all his benefits, who forgives all your iniquity, who heals all your diseases, who redeems your life from the Pit, who crowns you with steadfast love and mercy" (Psalm 103:2–4).

Prayer:

"O God who art the strength of Thy saints and who redeemest the souls of Thy servants: we bless Thy name for all those who have died in the Lord, and who now rest from their labors, having received the end of their faith, even the salvation of their souls. Especially we call to remembrance Thy loving kindness and Thy tender mercies to this Thy servant. For all Thy goodness that withheld not *his* portion in the joys of this earthly life, and for Thy guiding hand along the way of *his* pilgrimage, we give Thee thanks and praise. Especially we bless Thee for Thy grace that kindled in *his* heart the love of Thy dear name; that enabled *him* to fight the good fight unto the end, and to obtain the victory; yea, to become more than conqueror, through Him that loveth us. We magnify Thy holy name that *his* trials and temptations being ended, sickness and death being passed, with all the dangers and difficulties of this mortal life, *his* spirit is at home in Thy presence, at whose right hand dwelleth eternal peace. And grant, O Lord, we beseech Thee, that we who rejoice in the triumph of Thy saints may profit by their example, that becoming followers of their faith and patience, we also may enter with them into an inheritance incorruptible and undefiled, and that fadeth not away. Through Jesus Christ, our Lord, Amen."[2]

Meditation:

WHEN DEATH IS PRECIOUS

About A.D. 125 Aristides, the Greek scholar, explaining the success of Christianity, said, "If any righteous man among the Christians passes from the world, they rejoice and offer thanks to God and they escort his body with songs and thanksgiving as if he were setting out from one place to another nearby."

That is the spirit of this day. Sir Edward Jones attended the funeral of Robert Browning in Westminster Abbey, but he didn't like it. He knew this great poet, the virtues of his character, the abiding faith in his soul, the influence of his life, and he said the funeral was too sad and sombre. "I would have given something," he wrote, "for a banner or two to wave, and much more I would have given if a Chorister had come out of the triforium and rent the air with a trumpet."

Through the tears and saddened emotions of this day

should be a joyous optimism, sustained by the faith that "Precious in the sight of the Lord is the death of his saints" (Psalm 116:15).

The word precious means "of great value, very dear, highly esteemed." To say death is ever very dear, or of great value, or highly esteemed seems unthinkable, the comment of a hard heart, or the expression of a vengeance-seeking enemy. Most of us assume death to be the worst thing that could befall us. Death—we fear it, hide from it, attempt to evade it.

But the Scripture says, "precious, very dear, of great value, highly esteemed in the sight of the Lord is the death of his saints." Man and God look at events in different ways. God's outlook is not the same as man's. God sees the end of things from the beginning, while man sees only in part, through a glass dimly.

Note, however, not all deaths are precious. Some people disappoint God so! They mess up their lives so; they rebel against the Heavenly Father. When such a one dies without change, it grieves the heart of God.

I

Death is precious to God only when it comes to a saint. God longs for the fellowship of His children—and when death comes to them, and they are able to come to His side forever, it is a very dear experience, of great value—precious to Him. The very purpose of creation, of the universe and earthly life, is to develop saints worthy of eternal existence with God. Life is our trial run where we attempt to qualify; death is the promotion. Life is a school; death is the commencement.

A farmer cultivates his field, plants the seed, and eagerly tends it, then awaits the harvest when the kernel shall be separated from the stalk. The gospel seeds have been planted to grow and develop our souls in Christ's likeness. Death is the harvest time when the soul is separated from the outworn body—it is a time of rejoicing.

How pleased God must be today! I called in a home one evening where the only son had just returned from the front-line battlefields where he had been for nearly a year. From the dangers of that battle front, and the temptations of army life, he came home pure, safe, and sound. What a reunion! What tears of joy were shed! It was a precious homecoming. God is filled with joy as he welcomes a faithful soldier home, safe, unblemished and unharmed from the trials of earthly life.

II

Not only is death precious to God, but also to the saint. This is a day of victory. It is the crowning event of life, entry into the eternal Kingdom. "Eye hath not seen, nor ear heard, neither have entered into the heart of man, the things which God hath prepared for them [his saints] that love him" (I Corinthians 2:9).

O, it must be wonderful! Paul the Apostle longed to die saying, "For to me . . . to die is gain." He was in flesh only to serve God. An elderly lady said, "I am getting a bit anxious to take that journey."

THE VICTORS

They have triumphed who have died;
They have passed the porches wide,
Leading from the House of Night
To the splendid lawns of light,
They have gone on that far road
Leading to their new abode,
And from curtained casements we
Watch their going wistfully.

They have won, for they have read
The bright secrets of the dead;
And they gain the deep unknown,
Hearing Life's strange undertone.
In the race across the days
They are victors; theirs the praise,
Theirs the glory and the pride—
They have triumphed, having died![3]

It is worth working for, planning for, sacrificing for, and laying up treasures for. When you and I die, only one thing matters: not how much money we have, not how many flowers decorate the chancel, not how many people attend, not how many lodges we belonged to—only one thing—what is in your soul? How much of Jesus Christ is there? Are you in harmony with God? *What will it profit a man if he gains the whole world, and loses his own soul?*

Choral Anthem:

"Hallelujah Chorus"

Benediction:

Now our Lord Jesus Christ himself, and God, even our Father, which hath loved us, and hath given us everlasting consolation and good hope through grace, Comfort your hearts and establish you in every good word and work (II Thessalonians 2:16–17 AV).

Postlude:

"I Know That My Redeemer Liveth," from Handel's "Messiah"

"The Heavens Declare His Glory," Beethoven

XIX

For an Average Church Member

Prelude:

"Nearer My God to Thee"

Opening Scriptural Sentence:

"Fear not, for I have redeemed you; I have called you by name, you are mine. When you pass through the waters will be with you; and through the rivers, they shall not overwhelm you; when you walk through fire you shall not be burned, and the flame shall not consume you. For I am the Lord your God, the Holy One of Israel, your Savior . . (Isaiah 43:1–3).

Invocation:

Thou who art the God of the living; to whom there are no dead; in whose sight, those whom we call dead are still alive we offer thanks to Thee who giveth us the victory, through Him who lives, though He was dead; even Jesus Christ our Lord. Amen.

Hymn: (Optional) "O God, Our Help in Ages Past"

(This may be organ music, choral anthem, vocal solo, or spoken)

> O God, our help in ages past,
> Our hope for years to come,
> Our shelter from the stormy blast,
> And our eternal home.

Under the shadow of Thy throne
Thy saints have dwelt secure;
Sufficient is Thine arm alone,
And our defense is sure.

A thousand ages in Thy sight
Are like an evening gone,
Short as the watch that ends the night
Before the rising sun.

O God, our help in ages past,
Our hope for years to come,
Be Thou our guard while troubles last,
And our eternal home.[1]

Scripture Reading:

"But from there you will seek the Lord your God, and you will find him, if you search after him with all your heart and with all your soul. When you are in tribulation, and all these things come upon you in the latter days, you will return to the Lord your God and obey his voice, for the Lord your God is a merciful God; he will not fail you or destroy you or forget the covenant with your fathers which he swore to them" (Deuteronomy 4:29–31).

"The Lord is my light and my salvation; whom shall I fear? The Lord is the stronghold of my life; of whom shall I be afraid? . . . I believe that I shall see the goodness of the Lord in the land of the living! Wait for the Lord; be strong, and let your heart take courage; yea, wait for the Lord!" (Psalm 27:1, 13–14).

"And I heard a voice from heaven saying, 'Write this: Blessed are the dead who die in the Lord henceforth.' 'Blessed indeed,' says the Spirit, 'that they may rest from their labors, for their deeds follow them!'" (Revelation 14:13).

"Then he showed me the river of the water of life, bright

as crystal, flowing from the throne of God and of the La[mb]
through the middle of the street of the city; also, on eit[her]
side of the river, the tree of life with its twelve kinds of fr[uit]
yielding its fruit each month; and the leaves of the tree w[ere]
for the healing of the nations. There shall no more be a[ny]
thing accursed, but the throne of God and of the Lamb sh[all]
be in it, and his servants shall worship him; they shall see [his]
face, and his name shall be on their foreheads. And ni[ght]
shall be no more; they need no light of lamp or sun, for [the]
Lord God will be their light, and they shall reign for e[ver]
and ever" (Revelation 22:1–5).

Meditation:

THE GLORIOUS DAWN

Someone said at the time of bereavement, "I feel that [if I]
can believe in God, I shall have all I need." To be su[re]
faith in God is the sublimest and most comforting fact [in]
the world. Human explanations and words are often em[pty]
and frustrating at such an hour, but there is One who is ev[er]
lasting to everlasting, the Creator of life, the Planner [of]
death, the Provider of eternal habitation. At no time d[oes]
one feel more helpless than at death. Hence Amos urges [us]
to "Seek him that maketh the seven stars and Orion, a[nd]
turneth the shadow of death into the morning . . . T[he]
Lord is his name" (Amos 5:8, AV).

God alone can comfort you. Why is this so?

I

First, because He turns the shadows of suffering into [a]
glorious morning of rest. Have you ever been painfully s[ick]
in the darkness of night—you could get no comfort, find [no]
relief? Things always look worse and more frightening [at]
night. Then, the gentle rays of morning brightened the s[ky]

medical assistance was available, and you were able then to rest comfortably. What a glorious dawn!

After one has gone through the weariness of the flesh, and the suffering of a lingering illness, how wonderful it is that "he giveth his beloved sleep" (Psalm 127:2). God has brought through death a rest from the agony of a broken body and release from the hampering limitations of this world, for in Hebrews 4:9 one reads, "So then, there remains a sabbath rest for the people of God," and in Revelation 14:13 "Blessed are the dead, who die in the Lord henceforth . . . that they may rest from their labors," and in II Corinthians 5:8, "To be absent from the body, is to be present with the Lord." Romans 8:18 AV, ". . . the sufferings of this present time are not worthy to be compared with the glory which shall be revealed in us."

II

God can comfort you also, because He turns the shadow of death into the glorious morning of life. In Old Testament times people groped for life after death, but were never certain of it. However, the glorious news of the gospel is that death is not the end. We live on the right side of one tremendous historical testimony, the fact that Jesus Christ, who though He died, yet lived to be seen by hundreds of different people on many different occasions. "Because I live," He said, "you shall live also. . . ." "Jesus Christ has abolished death, and brought life and immortality to life. . . ." "I am the resurrection, and the life; he that believeth in me, though he were dead, yet shall he live."

In ancient times, mourners buried loved ones facing the west, toward the sunset, the darkness, the night. But after Christ arose from the dead, Christians bury loved ones facing the east, toward the sunrise, the light, the dawn of the day.

III

God comforts you also by turning the shadows of disappointed hopes into the morning of rewards. This earthly life is filled with disappointments, heartaches, frustrations, unfulfilled dreams. Death is the gateway to a world of rewards, more valuable than all the fame, money, recognition, joy and friendship which this world can ever give. "Eye hath not seen, nor ear heard, neither have entered into the heart of man, the things which God hath prepared for them that love him" (I Corinthians 2:9 AV). Often our work for the Lord on earth is seemingly unnoticed, unappreciated, and vain. It is not so; instead the promise of our Lord is, "If any man's work abide . . . he shall receive a reward" (I Corinthians 3:14, AV). "God is not unrighteous to forget your work and labour of love" (Hebrews 6:10, AV). "Blessed are the dead which die in the Lord . . . their works do follow them" (Revelation 14:13, AV).

Marshal Foch, the French general in World War I, said to the minister attending him at death, "I have had my span of life. All I want now is heaven."

The prayer of one aged believer was, "Lord, now lettest thou thy servant depart in peace, according to thy word; for mine eyes have seen thy salvation" (Luke 2:29–30). God alone can turn the shadows of your night into sunrise tomorrow.

Prayer:

O God, who art from everlasting to everlasting: though our hearts are full, we look through the shadows and clouds hovering about us to see Thy light of love and mercy and hope. Our trust is in Thee. We thank Thee for the promise that in the severing of this physical tie, the spirit has been released from the pain and infirmities of a weakened body, and that which has brought us bereavement has meant peace and life and victory to the departed. We thank Thee for the assurance of that abode where pain shall be no more, and tears shall be wiped from their eyes, and death will be unknown. Oh Lord, how wonderful it must be "that eye hath not seen, nor ear heard, nor has it entered into the heart of man what thou hast promised for those who love thee"—and into which inheritance our departed has already entered.

We thank Thee for *her* life, rich in faith and good works, esteemed by *her* family, friends, community and church. We hold in tender memory *her* steady forbearance, quiet patience in suffering. Sustain and comfort *her* family with the consolation that in Thy holy keeping are the living and the dead; and all are safe until Thou shall reunite us in an everlasting love. In loneliness, steady *her* companion of many years. Give us strength to return to our duties until the summons comes when we shall say, "Father, I have finished the work which thou gavest me to do" and He shall say, "Well done, good and faithful servant. Enter into thy joy." Amen.

Hymn: (Optional) "Hark, Hark, My Soul!"

(This may be organ music, choral anthem, vocal solo, or spoken)

> Hark, hark, my soul! angelic songs are swelling
> O'er earth's green fields and ocean's wave-beat shore;
> How sweet the truth those blessed strains are telling
> Of that new life when sin shall be no more!
>
> *Chorus:*
> Angels of Jesus, angels of light,
> Singing to welcome the pilgrims of the night!
>
> Far, far away, like bells at evening pealing,
> The voice of Jesus sounds o'er land and sea,

And laden souls by thousands meekly stealing,
Kind Shepherd, turn their weary steps to Thee.

Onward we go, for still we hear them singing,
"Come, weary souls, for Jesus bids you come";
And through the dark, its echoes sweetly ringing,
The music of the gospel leads us home.

Angels, sing on, your faithful watches keeping;
Sing us sweet fragments of the songs above:
Till morning's joy shall end the night of weeping,
And life's long shadows break in cloudless love.[2]

Benediction:

The grace of our Lord Jesus Christ, the love of God, and the communion of the Holy Spirit be with us all to the end, and in the end. Amen.

Postlude:

"Blest Be the Tie"

XX

For a Person of Advanced Age

Prelude:

"Rock of Ages"
"Peace, Perfect Peace"
"One Sweetly Solemn Thought"

Opening Scriptural Sentence:

"Lord, thou hast been our dwelling place in all generations. Before the mountains were brought forth, or ever thou
hadst formed the earth and the world, even from everlasting to everlasting thou art God" (Psalm 90:1–2).

Invocation:

Merciful Father, who art Strength to the weak, Refresh-
ment to the weary, Comfort to the sad, Help to the tempted,
and Life to the dying: make us, we pray Thee, sensitive to
the presence of Thy comfort in accordance with our Lord's
assurance that we will not be left alone, and grant us the
faith of the prophets who could see, in approaching the
shades of night, the promise of glorious sunrise through
Jesus Christ, our Lord. Amen.

Hymn: (Optional) "For All the Saints Who from Their La-
    bors Rest"

(This may be organ music, choral anthem, vocal solo, or
spoken)

> For all the saints, who from their labors rest,
> Who Thee by faith before the world confessed,
> Thy name, O Jesus, be forever blessed.
>   Alleluia!
>
> Thou wast their rock, their fortress, and their might;
> Thou, Lord, their captain in the well-fought fight;
> Thou, in the darkness drear, the one true light
>   Alleluia!
>
> O blest communion, fellowship divine.
> We feebly struggle; they in glory shine;
> Yet all are one in Thee, for all are Thine.
>   Alleluia!

The golden evening brightens in the west;
Soon, soon to faithful warriors cometh rest;
Sweet is the calm of Paradise, the blest.
Alleluia![1]

(Other appropriate hymn: "When on My Day of Life")

Scripture Reading:

"I lift up my eyes to the hills. From whence does my help come? My help comes from the Lord, who made heaven and earth. He will not let your foot be moved, he who keeps you will not slumber. Behold, he who keeps Israel will neither slumber nor sleep. The Lord is your keeper; the Lord is your shade on your right hand. The sun shall not smite you by day, nor the moon by night. The Lord will keep you from all evil; he will keep your life. The Lord will keep your going out and your coming in from this time forth and for evermore" (Psalm 121).

"Who shall separate us from the love of Christ? Shall tribulation, or distress, or persecution, or famine, or nakedness, or peril, or sword? . . . No, in all these things we are more than conquerors through him who loved us. For I am sure that neither death, nor life, nor angels, nor principalities, nor things present, nor things to come, nor powers, nor height, nor depth, nor anything else in all creation, will be able to separate us from the love of God in Christ Jesus our Lord" (Romans 8:35, 37–39).

Prayer:

Almighty God, who art like the sky that bends above us, and surrounds all the earth; who art the true and lasting light which shines even in the times of our shadow and darkness; look upon Thy children with constant mercy, and give us a spirit of understanding promised by Thy dear Son.

When our eyes no longer behold what we have loved, and when we listen for footsteps of those who have gone from our sight and hear them not, we can but turn to Thee.

We thank Thee for this life which has come to its final change. May it still be an inspiration and guide. May these who have been loved by *her,* keep in mind that they must love and serve Thee more because *she* is not here. May they show their love for *her* by doing things *she* loved the best. May they be gentler, kinder, more thoughtful, thus to compensate for *her* loss.

Help us to be grateful for Thine eternal love which summons souls to rest from their labors, and dost permit them at eventide to enter into Thy peace. Amid the changes of this world, make us strong and calm, eager to serve, more inclined to love, and persuade us that neither death nor life, nor things present, nor things to come, shall be able to separate us from the love of God which is in Christ Jesus our Lord. Amen.

Hymn: (Optional) "Abide with Me"

(This may be organ music, choral anthem, vocal solo, or spoken)

> Abide with me; fast falls the eventide;
> The darkness deepens; Lord, with me abide;
> When other helpers fail, and comforts flee,
> Help of the helpless, O abide with me.
>
> Swift to its close ebbs out life's little day;
> Earth's joys grow dim, its glories pass away;
> Change and decay in all around I see;
> O Thou, who changest not, abide with me.
>
> I need Thy presence every passing hour;
> What but Thy grace can foil the tempter's power?
> Who like Thyself my guide and stay can be?
> Through cloud and sunshine, O abide with me.

Hold Thou Thy cross before my closing eyes;
Shine through the gloom, and point me to the skies;
Heaven's morning breaks, and earth's vain shadows flee;
In life, in death, O Lord, abide with me.[2]

Meditation:

THE BEAUTY OF THE SUNSET

Have you ever sat on a hill and watched the sun going down—and has your soul thrilled at the beauty of the sunset? That is what I want you to see in this death today. I like to think of this world as a park filled with gardens and playgrounds, trees and lakes, museums and swimming pools. We are like children privileged to spend a day in the great park. The time we are privileged to spend is not the same in length, in light, nor in beauty. Some days are long and sunlit, others are cloudy and stormy, as in a winter's tale. Some children are able to stay only a few short hours. Some must go home at noon of day while the sun is still shining. Others stay till the sun begins to set in the beauty of the west. For each of us the moment comes when the great nurse, Death, takes us by the hand and quietly says, "It is time to go home, my child; come, come with me." This one has been privileged to live until the shadows of the setting sun had lengthened, and the evening had come; the business of the world was hushed, and the fever of life was over, and work was done. Oh, the beauty of the sunset of a life like this.

I

It is a beautiful death, because it climaxes a wonderful life. One need not eulogize the character of the departed to you who have known *her*—*her* life tells its own story. The friendships expressed here demonstrate *her* influence; *her* family tells something about the quality of life.

Some there are who come to the end of life filled with remorse and regret. "Take my wasted years," said one, "and bury them with me." He had misused his life, had furthered no great cause of human welfare, had buried his talents in cheap, selfish security. To such the Master said, "Thou wicked and slothful servant," and instructed that they be cast into outer darkness.

The sweetest words which one could ever hear, the most beautiful benediction that could conclude a life, the most coveted epitaph that could grace one's farewell, would be those words spoken by the Master when He said, "Well done, thou good and faithful servant: thou hast been faithful over a few things, I will make thee ruler over many things: enter thou into the joy of thy Lord."

The one we honor lived a useful, devoted, unselfish life. The world has been made better for *her* having lived. The Kingdom of Heaven has been strengthened by *her* efforts. Surely, the congratulatory hand of life's all-wise Judge reaches out to the accompaniment, "Well done, thou good and faithful servant."

II

This is a beautiful death also, because it comes as a friend to old age. I really mean that. We often wish in a childish way that life would never end, and in our rebellious moments we wonder why God created the universe so death comes at all. We feel death is an enemy of life—and not a friend.

But that is not right. It is the knowledge that our years are limited that makes them so precious. Plato was right when he declared that infinite life on this earth for us human beings would not be desirable even if it were possible. Who would want to live a never-ending existence on earth through endless years of struggle and revolution, pain and worry, conflict and labor—with no possibility of escape? Life would be so monotonous and boring with no heights or depths, without crescendos or diminuendos, with no challenge nor achievement. What drudgery if day would never end, and the sun would never set.

Have you toiled through the hot, sweaty, sweltering day, looking forward to the sunset? Time moved so slowly; it seemed the day would never end. Then, when evening finally came—how welcome, what cool peace and embracing rest; what satisfying release, what a wonderful friend.

This one has lived many years, and death must have come as a friend indeed.

III

Then, this is a beautiful death because there are rays of promise for a better tomorrow.

> O happy soul, be thankful now, and rest!
>   Heaven is a goodly land;
> And God is love; and those He loves are blest;
>   Now thou dost understand
> The least thou hast is better than the best
> That thou didst hope for; now upon thine eyes
>   The new life opens fair;
> Before thy feet the blessed journey lies
>   Through homelands everywhere;
> And heaven to thee is all a sweet surprise.[3]

The best is yet to be. Death is not the end; it is only a new beginning. It is going to bed on a cold, black night, and waking with the sun always shining.

Victor Hugo, the French author, wrote, "When I go down to the grave, I can say, like many others, 'I have finished my day's work.' But I cannot say, 'I have finished my life.' My day's work will begin the next morning. The tomb is not a blind alley; it is a thoroughfare. It closes on the twilight, and opens on the dawn."

Rev. Robert J. Burdette, shortly before his death, wrote a personal letter to the editor of an Eastern paper, saying: "I watch the sunset as I look out over the rim of the blue Pacific, and there is no mystery beyond the horizon line, because I know what there is over there. I have been there. I have journeyed in those lands. Over there where the sun is sinking is Japan. That star is rising over China. In that direction lie the Philippines. I know all that. Well, there is another land that I look toward as I watch the sunset. I have never seen it. I have never seen anyone who has been there, but it has a more abiding reality than any of these lands which I know. This land beyond the sunset, this land of immortality, this fair and blessed country of the soul—why, this heaven of ours is the one thing in the world which I know with absolute, unshaken, unchangeable certainty. This I know with a knowledge that is never shadowed by a passing cloud of doubt. I may not always be certain about this world; my geographical locations may sometimes become confused, but the other world—that I know. And as the afternoon sun sinks lower, faith shines more clearly and hope, lifting her voice in a higher key, sings the songs of fruition. My work is about ended, I think. The best of it I have done poorly; any of it I might have done better, but I have done it. And in a fairer land, with finer material, and a better working light, I will do better work."[4]

> Sunset and evening star,
>   And one clear call for me!
> And may there be no moaning of the bar,
>   When I put out to sea,

But such a tide as moving seems asleep,
　　Too full for sound and foam,
When that which drew from out the boundless deep
　　Turns again home.

Twilight and evening bell,
　　And after that the dark!
And may there be no sadness of farewell,
　　When I embark;

For tho' from out our bourne of Time and Place
　　The flood may bear me far,
I hope to see my Pilot face to face
　　When I have crossed the bar.[5]

Benediction:

"O Lord, support us all the day long of our troublous life until the shadows lengthen and the evening comes, and the busy world is hushed, and the fever of life is over, and our work is done. Then in Thy mercy grant us a safe lodging and a holy rest, and peace at the last. Amen."[6]

Postlude:

"Now the Day Is Over"

XXI

For an Unchurched Person

Prelude:

"There's a Wideness in God's Mercy" (Emmelar)
"When Thou Art Near"
"Nearer, My God, to Thee"

Opening Scriptural Sentence:

"Thou dost keep him in perfect peace, whose mind is stayed on thee, because he trusts in thee" (Isaiah 26:3).

Invocation:

Eternal God, and Heavenly Father, from whom we have come, and to whom our spirits return: help us to wait before Thee with reverent and submissive hearts, that as we listen to the Scriptures beautifully written and meaningfully read, we may be lifted above our darkness and distress into the comfort and peace of Thy presence; through Jesus Christ, the Lord. Amen.

Scripture Reading:

"Hear, O Lord, when I cry aloud, be gracious to me and answer me! Thou hast said, 'Seek ye my face.' My heart says to thee, 'Thy face, Lord, do I seek.' Hide not thy face from me. Turn not thy servant away in anger, thou who hast been my help. Cast me not off, forsake me not, O God of my salvation! For my father and my mother have forsaken me, but the Lord will take me up. Teach me thy way, O Lord; and lead me on a level path because of my enemies" (Psalm 27:7–11).

"But do not ignore this one fact, beloved, that with the Lord one day is as a thousand years, and a thousand years as one day. The Lord is not slow about his promise as some count slowness, but is forbearing toward you, not wishing that any should perish, but that all should reach repentance. But the day of the Lord will come like a thief, and then the heavens will pass away with a loud noise, and the elements will be dissolved with fire, and the earth and the works that are upon it will be burned up. Since all these things are thus to be dissolved, what sort of persons ought you to be in live·

of holiness and godliness, waiting for and hastening the coming of the day of God, because of which the heavens will be kindled and dissolved, and the elements will melt with fire! But according to his promise we wait for new heavens and a new earth in which righteousness dwells. Therefore, beloved since you wait for these, be zealous to be found by him without spot or blemish, and at peace" (II Peter 3: 8–14).

Hymn: (Optional) "There's a Wideness in God's Mercy"

(This may be organ music, choral anthem, vocal solo, or spoken)

> There's a wideness in God's mercy,
> Like the wideness of the sea;
> There's a kindness in His justice,
> Which is more than liberty.
>
> For the love of God is broader
> Than the measure of man's mind;
> And the heart of the Eternal
> Is most wonderfully kind.
>
> If our love were but more simple,
> We should take Him at His word,
> And our lives would be all sunshine
> In the sweetness of our Lord.[1]

Meditation:

BEYOND SORROW

My remarks upon this solemn occasion, when we meet to pay tribute to your loved one, shall be very brief. Brief because words alone do not brighten or tarnish the future—one's life and faith determine his destiny. Brief because at such a time none of us is able to express what he really feels.

Words are inadequate to convey our full measure of sorrow.

Today, we stand face to face with the two great mysteries of the universe—life and death. A few hours ago this body had life; now, although it has the same chemical constituents, life is gone. God alone knows the meaning of life and death.

People quite naturally are saddened by death. Because of our fears, uncertainty, personal loneliness, and lack of faith, we are reluctant for death to invade our circle of friends. That reluctance was expressed by Voltaire who, having spent a life of blasphemy, said to his physician on his deathbed, "I'll give you all my fortune if you'll give me six months to live." The Queen of Scots loved life so much that she cried, "I'll give you all my kingdom for one more minute to live." Life—we love it, cling to it, fight for it. Death—we fear it.

Today, in the midst of such an experience, may we turn to the words of Jesus to His disciples when speaking about His coming death: ". . . you will be sorrowful, but your sorrow will turn to joy" (John 16:20). To be sure, the resurrection turned their fear into faith, their sorrow into joy, and their doubts into certainty. The same can happen to you.

What is life?

Life is a school. Death is the commencement. If we have prepared our spirits well, we will be promoted.

"All the world's a stage," said Shakespeare. We are actors who play our part and disappear. The curtain falls and all is over. If we have played our parts well, the Great Director has a great future in store.

Life is a testing road. The test ended, the road leads into a new state of existence.

Life, says James the Apostle, is a vapor that appeareth for a time and then vanishes away, like a cloud floating through the air, which finally changes to a different form of liquid.

Sir Walter Raleigh called life a journey, like a ship at sea that sails on and on. We see it going, going, going, until it drifts out of sight into another land.

> When men go down to the sea in ships
> 'Tis not to the sea they go;
> Some isle or pole the mariner's goal.
> And thither they sail through calm and gale,
> When down to the sea they go.
>
> When souls go down to the sea by ship
>   And the dark ship's name is Death,
> Why mourn and wail at the vanishing sail?
> Though outward bound, God's world is round,
>   And only a ship is Death.
>
> When I go down to the sea by ship,
>   And Death unfurls her sail,
> Weep not for me, for there will be
> A living host on another coast
>   To beckon and cry, "All Hail!"[2]

Another has said, "Life is a game we play with our fellow men; the rules are stamped in the universe." When the game is over, and:

> . . . when the One Great Scorer comes,
>   To write against your name,
> He writes—not that you won or lost—
>   But how you played the game.[3]

Furthermore,

> My life is but a weaving
>   Between my Lord and me;
> I may not choose the colors,
>   He knows what they should be;
> For He can view the pattern
>   Upon the upper side,

While I can see it only
  On this, the under side.

Sometimes He weaveth sorrow,
  Which seems strange to me;
But I will trust His judgment,
  And work as faithfully;
'Tis He who fills the shuttle,
  He knows just what is best,
So I shall weave in earnest
  And leave with Him the rest.

Not till the loom is silent
  And the shuttles cease to fly
Shall God unroll the canvas
  And explain the reason why—
The dark threads are as needful
  In the weaver's skillful hand
As the threads of gold and silver
  In the pattern He has planned.[4]

Death, you see, is not an unforeseen accident; not something left out of the scheme of our Creator. Rather it is
something well planned and necessary in the sight of God.
It is an appointed event that will irresistibly come to you.
"He that hath the Son hath [eternal] life; and he that hath
not the Son of God hath not [eternal] life (I John 5:12, AV).
Weep not over this one who passes into the beyond, but see
that you are prepared.

Prayer:

O Thou, who wast before all time, and will endure beyond the end of all things; who art more lasting than the
rocks which have endured through the generations, or the
ancient hills that look down upon thousands of generations,
or the sun, moon and stars that shine upon man: we bow
reverently before Thee. We know in our deepest thoughts,

beneath our doubts and fears, that Thou art great. Give us also the confidence that Thou art good and that Thou "forgivest all our iniquities." Give us a true perspective of faith in which to view life in all its relationships. Help us to discern the invisible realities behind the fleeting shadows of sense and time.

O Thou who art able to guide the suns in their courses, mould the mountain ranges, and bring life to birth—we present to Thee this our loved one.

Benediction:

May almighty God, the Father, the Son, and the Holy Spirit, bless you and keep you, now and forevermore. Amen.

Postlude:

"Abide with Me"

"Elegy" (Franz Schubert)

XXII
For a Person of Another Religion

Prelude:

"Traumerei" (Robert Schumann)

"When Thou Art Near " (Bach)

Opening Scriptural Sentence:

"The eternal God is your dwelling place, and underneath are the everlasting arms" (Deuteronomy 33:27).

Invocation:

O Thou who dost walk with us in the midday, become our assuring companion in this midnight hour as well. Lift our eyes beyond the shadows of the earth, and enable us to put our trust in Thee, we pray, for Thy name's sake. Amen.

Hymn: (Optional) "There's a Wideness in God's Mercy"

(This may be organ music, choral anthem, vocal solo, or spoken)

> There's a wideness in God's mercy,
> Like the wideness of the sea;
> There's a kindness in His justice;
> Which is more than liberty.
>
> There is welcome for the sinner,
> And more graces for the good;
> There is mercy with the Saviour;
> There is healing in His blood.
>
> For the love of God is broader
> Than the measure of man's mind,
> And the heart of the Eternal
> Is most wonderfully kind.
>
> If our love were but more simple,
> We should take Him at His word;
> And our lives would be all sunshine
> In the sweetness of our Lord.[1]

Scripture Reading:

"When I look at thy heavens, the work of thy fingers, the moon and the stars which thou hast established; what is man that thou art mindful of him, and the son of man that thou dost care for him? Yet thou hast made him little less than God, and dost crown him with glory and honor. Thou hast given him dominion over the works of thy hands; thou hast put all things under his feet, all sheep and oxen, and also the beasts of the field, the birds of the air, and the fish of the sea, whatever passes along the paths of the sea" (Psalm 8:3–8).

"Are not five sparrows sold for two pennies? And not one of them is forgotten before God. Why, even the hairs of your head are all numbered. Fear not; you are of more value than many sparrows" (Luke 12:6–7).

"But some one will ask, 'How are the dead raised? With what kind of body do they come?' You foolish man! What you sow does not come to life unless it dies. . . . So is it with the resurrection of the dead. What is sown is perishable, what is raised is imperishable. It is sown in dishonor, it is raised in glory. It is sown in weakness, it is raised in power. It is sown a physical body, it is raised a spiritual body. If there is a physical body, there is also a spiritual body" (I Corinthians 15:35–36, 42–44).

"Truly, truly, I say to you, he who hears my word and believes him who sent me, has eternal life; he does not come into judgment, but has passed from death to life" (John 5:24).

Meditation:

THE MOST IMPORTANT QUESTIONS EVER ASKED

There are two fundamental questions which come to us at a time such as this. First: Is life after death reasonable? Second: Is it desirable?

I

The age-old question has always been, "If a man die, shall he live again?" (Job 14:14). The Christian answer is, "Yes." Sir Arthur Keith, the British scientist, once said, "When a man dies, he goes out like a candle." Whereupon Professor

Compton replied, "The candle does not go out; its energy goes on and on to the farthest reaches of the universe."

Yes, the most reasonable faith in this universe is a belief in life after death. God who gave birth to our existence, who made us spiritual souls in His image, who permits us to develop into self-conscious sons and daughters and capable personalities, who permits us to dream dreams of life that has no end—would not terminate our growth. If human personalities are the most precious things in this universe, and Jesus taught that they were, and if our existence is so carefully planned that the very hairs of our head are known and numbered, would God let us live our few years on earth and then snuff us out as one blows out a candle? Would it make sense to suppose that in all His efforts in creating His universe, that God would suddenly turn around and blot out His most delicate creation? If you watched a skilled craftsman spend twenty years in fashioning a particular fine watch, would you expect him to set it to run a few minutes and then crash it to bits beneath his heel? No, such would be unreasonable.

Alfred Swan testifies, "Without immortality nothing is intelligible; with immortality, everything is." As Paul says, "Now we see through a glass darkly; but then face to face: now I know in part; but then shall I know even as I am known" (I Corinthians 13:12, AV). Again, "This corruptible must put on incorruption, and this mortal must put on immortality" (I Corinthians 15:53, AV). Yes, universal reason demands it; universal desire demands it; universal justice demands it; universal faith demands it.

But it is more than reasonable, it is certain. Jesus, whose integrity was beyond question and who founded the purest system of religion and ethics, said, ". . . if it were not so, I would have told you" (John 14:2, AV). In fact His resur-

rection vindicates the certainty of the truth. Christ ꞏ
scended into the grave, and like Samson of old, tore ap
the pillars of the temple of death and triumphantly p
claimed, "I am the resurrection, and the life; he that beli
eth in me, though he were dead, yet shall he live: And wh
soever liveth and believeth in me shall never die . .
(John 11:25–26).

II

The second question, "Is life after death desirable?" Wh
is the future life like? All of us would like to know m
about it, but fortunately we do not. Even Jesus did not
everything about it.

Whether such an existence is desirable depends entir
upon our relationship to God while on earth. If one is livi
an evil life now, the future life will be more and more h
ish even during eternity, unless one changes. One who
living a godly life on earth, who is most concerned abc
his neighbors and the underprivileged, one who takes an ꞏ
tive part in the Kingdom of God, who opens his heart
Christ and becomes more and more like Him, who p
heaven within his home, community and world—he w
find the future life increasingly happy. He will be ever m
joyful, more useful, more like Jesus Christ. When such a ꞏ
lays aside his worn-out body, he sets the spirit free; he kee
on growing and developing. It is a place where love finds
own, where beauty, peace, happiness, and justice reign.
came that they may have life, and have it abundantl
(John 10:10).

Prayer:

O Thou who art the Creator of our dying bodies, and
Father of our undying souls, who dost one by one gatl
Thy scattered children from the distraction of time to

peace of eternity, out of the earthly life into the unknown future—we bow before Thee.

We thank Thee that deep in the human heart is the unquenchable trust that life does not end with death, but that Thou dost care for us.

O Thou who art a Helper of the helpless, unite the bereaved, we pray, with the bonds of undying love. May the memory of their loved one strengthen their faith, hope, and love. May this experience chasten desires, better aspirations; bring truer diligence, less trust in ourselves and more in Thee. May these friends find peace in Thee, our Strength and Redeemer.

Benediction:

"Unto him that is able to do exceeding abundantly above all that we ask or think . . . Unto him be glory . . . throughout all ages, world without end. Amen" (Ephesians 3:20, 21).

Postlude:

"It Singeth Low in Every Heart" (Henry Hills)
"Faith" (Mendelssohn)

XXIII
For Multiple Funerals or General Use

Prelude:

"Prelude in E Minor" (Chopin)
"Still, Still with Thee"

Opening Scriptural Sentence:

"God is our refuge and strength, a very present help in trouble. Therefore we will not fear . . ." (Psalm 46:1–2).

Invocation:

Ever-living God, before whose face pass the generations of men, whose mercies are from everlasting to everlasting, Thou hast taught that in quietness and confidence shall be our strength: by the power of Thy Spirit, lift us to Thy presence, where we may be still and know that Thou art God, through Jesus Christ the Lord. Amen.

Hymn: (Optional) "There Is No Sorrow, Lord, Too Light"

(This may be organ music, choral anthem, vocal solo, or spoken)

> There is no sorrow, Lord, too light
> To bring in prayer to Thee;
> There is no anxious care too slight
> To wake Thy sympathy.
>
> Thou, who hast trod the thorny road,
> Wilt share each small distress;
> The love which bore the greater load
> Will not refuse the less.
>
> There is no secret sigh we breathe
> But meets Thine ear divine;
> And every cross grows light beneath
> The shadow, Lord, of Thine.[1]

(Other appropriate hymns: "Lead Kindly Light," "There's a Wideness in God's Mercy," "Sunset and Evening Star")

Scripture Reading:

"Lord, thou hast been our dwelling place in all generations. Before the mountains were brought forth, or ever thou hadst formed the earth and the world, from everlasting to everlasting thou art God. Thou turnest man back to the dust, and sayest, 'Turn back, O children of men!' For a thousand years in thy sight are but as yesterday when it is past, or as a watch in the night. Thou dost sweep men away; they are like a dream, like grass which is renewed in the morning; in the morning it flourishes and is renewed; in the evening it fades and withers. . . . The years of our life are three-score and ten . . . yet their span is but toil and trouble; they are soon gone, and we fly away. . . . So teach us to number our days that we may get a heart of wisdom" (Psalm 90:1–6, 10, 12).

"Blessed are the poor in spirit, for theirs is the kingdom of heaven. Blessed are those who mourn, for they shall be comforted. Blessed are the meek, for they shall inherit the earth. Blessed are those who hunger and thirst for righteousness, for they shall be satisfied. Blessed are the merciful, for they shall obtain mercy. Blessed are the pure in heart, for they shall see God. Blessed are the peacemakers, for they shall be called sons of God. Blessed are those who are persecuted for righteousness' sake, for theirs is the kingdom of heaven. Blessed are you when men revile you and persecute you and utter all kinds of evil against you falsely on my account. Rejoice and be glad, for your reward is great in heaven, for so men persecuted the prophets who were before you. You are the salt of the earth; but if salt has lost its taste, how shall its saltness be restored? It is no longer good for anything except to be thrown out and trodden under foot by men. You are the light of the world. A city set on a hill cannot be hid. Nor do men light a lamp and put it under a bushel, but on a stand, and it gives light to all in the house. Let your light so shine before men, that they may see your good works and give glory to your Father who is in heaven" (Matthew 5:3–16).

Meditation:

THANK GOD FOR EVERY REMEMBRANCE

Dear friends: We have come together today for three distinct purposes.

First, we have come to express our mutual appreciation for the life of ——. Death depreciates life, and all too often our comrades are soon forgotten. Fittingly therefore, as a company of friends, we gathered to pay honest tribute, genuine appreciation, and to think upon *his* good qualities. Our departed *brother* had many noble and commendable characteristics. All of us have a sense of loss and feel a mutual sorrow. I do not mean to imply that our *brother* was perfect; the world has known only One such a person. Nor am I here determining *his* destiny. Rather, in the words of the Apostle Paul, "Whatever is true, whatever is honorable, whatever is just, whatever is pure, whatever is lovely, whatever is gracious, if there is any excellence, if there is anything worthy of praise, think about these things" (Philippians 4:8). To his friend Philemon, the Apostle wrote, "I thank my God always when I remember you . . ." (Philemon 3). Just so, we lift to God our gratitude for every remembrance of our departed.

We have come here, secondly, to unify and convey our sympathetic understanding to the bereaved family. Death is a separator that drops a curtain of silence between loved ones and friends. But today we are drawn together in a company to express our sympathy, to give strength and comfort to the distressed, and to make it known that we remember with loving concern.

The old Greeks, in whose language our New Testament was written, discovered that if a person really cared about the circumstances of his fellows, he might enter vicariously into that person's experience. They called this "synpathos," meaning "with suffering," from which comes our word "sympathy." By means of sympathy we enter into the minds and hearts of those who suffer, to share this sorrow. The old Latins, in whose language most of the history of the early church was written, discovered that when sympathy was sincere, a miracle resulted in the bereaved. They called it "con-fortis," meaning "together strong," and from it comes our word, "comfort."

Our sincere sympathy we extend together. May it bring the family comfort. Often I have heard folks say, "We could not have gone through it without the support of our friends."

> My greatest joy on earth shall be,
> To find at the turning of every road,
> The strong hand of a comrade kind,
> To help me onward with my load.
>
> But since I have no gold to give
> And only love can make amends,
> My daily prayer in life shall be,
> "God make me worthy of my friends."[2]

However, when human strength comes to an end, you are never alone, for there is an invisible companion, a Heavenly Father, who promises, "My peace I leave with you. . . ."

Finally, we have come to re-affirm our belief in immortality. "It is the end of life for which the first was made." "Without immortality, nothing is intelligible; with immortality, everything is." Life does not end at the grave! This is the great affirmation of the Christian faith! ". . . if our earthly house of this tabernacle were dissolved, we have a building of God, an house not made with hands, eternal in the heavens. . . ." "In my Father's house are many mansions. . . ." Thanks be unto "our Savior Jesus Christ who . . . brought life and immortality to light. . . ." Death is not what we have thought it to be at all. It is closing the door to earth and opening the door to heaven. It is putting off an old suit and dressing in a beautiful new garment. Death is going to sleep on a cold, wintry night and waking to find the sun always shining.

An anxious person once asked Bishop Berggrav of Norway, for an explanation of death. The Bishop told this story in reply: "One day a peasant took his little son with him on a visit to a village some distance away. Along the road they came to a swift stream which was spanned by a rickety old bridge. But it was daylight and the father and son made the crossing without mishap. . . . It was dusk when the two started their homeward journey. The boy remembered the stream and the old bridge, and became frightened. How would they be able to cross that turbulent water in the dark? His father, noticing his anxiety, lifted him up, and carried him in his arms. The fear subsided immediately, and before the boy knew it he was fast asleep on his father's shoulder. . . . As the sun of a new day streamed through the window of his bedroom, the boy awoke and discovered that he was safe at home."[3] Death is like that. What we fear most, the river of death, we cross unafraid if we fall asleep in Jesus. Then we shall awake in our Father's house of many mansions, where there is no night and no fear.

Prayer:

"Almighty God, who knowest our frame and rememberest that we are dust; look in Thy great compassion upon us, who have been brought into the presence of sorrow, and under the dark shadow of death. In the silence of this hour, speak to us of eternal things; and when our spirits sink before the mystery of life and of death, comfort us with the assurance that neither life nor death can ever separate us from Thy love, which is in Christ Jesus our Lord.

Most merciful God, the consolation of the sorrowful, look down in love and pity, we beseech Thee, upon Thy servants, whose joy is turned into mourning; so that, while they mourn, they may not be hopeless, but, remembering all Thy mercies, Thy promises, and Thy love in Christ, may give themselves into Thy hands to be taught and further led by Thee.

God of the spirits of all flesh, most humbly and heartily we thank Thee today for the great hope of eternal life which Thou hast given us in the gospel of Thy dear Son, Jesus Christ, and confirmed to us by His glorious resurrection from the grave; for His promises to them that fall asleep in Him, and who are forever with Him; for the revelation of that world where there is no more pain, and where parting is unknown; and for the assurance that in our Father's house are many mansions, and that those who sleep in Jesus the Lord will bring with Him.

Cheered by these hopes, we would commit our beloved dead into Thy holy and most merciful keeping, believing that, though we see them no more, they are safe with Thee; and they rest from their labors, and their works do follow them; through Jesus Christ our Lord."[4]

Benediction:

Unto whom, be glory and majesty, dominion and power both now and ever. Amen.

Postlude:

"Jerusalem, the Golden" (Alexander Ewing)

"Blest Be the Tie"

Burial Service for a Christian

Graveside Scripture:

"I know that my Redeemer lives, and at last he will stand upon the earth . . . then without my flesh I shall see God, whom I shall see on my side, and my eyes shall behold, and not another" (Job 19:25–27).

"Our light affliction, which is but for a moment, worketh for us a far more exceeding and eternal weight of glory. While we look not at the things which are seen, but at the things which are not seen: for the things which are seen are temporal; but the things which are not seen are eternal" (II Corinthians 4:17–18, AV).

Graveside Committal:

Cherishing memories which are forever sacred, sustained by a faith that is stronger than death, comforted by the hope of a life that shall endless be, all that is mortal of our friend we therefore commit to its resting place, amidst these beautiful surroundings of nature, in the assurance that if the earthly house of our tabernacle be dissolved, we have a building from God, a house not made with hands, eternal in the heavens.

Graveside Prayer:

By memory of the empty tomb of Him whom we call our Lord: by recollection of His words that bid us think of death as victory, and by our deathless love of dear ones gone, O God, may we perceive in the darkness through which we pass, the shadow of Thy hand, outstretched in love. To Thee there are no dead: in Thy sight, those we call dead are still alive. Thanks be to God who giveth us the victory, through Him who lived, though He was dead, even Jesus Christ, our Lord.

Graveside Benediction:

"Now the God of peace . . . Make you perfect in every good work to do his will . . . through Jesus Christ; to whom be glory for ever and ever. Amen" (Hebrews 13:20–21, AV).

Burial Service for a Non-Christian

Graveside Committal:

Again we are called on to assemble in this beautiful city of the dead, hallowed by the sacred memory of its inhabitants. Here, around us, in that peace which the world cannot give or take away, lie the mortal remains of unnumbered dead. Stones and monuments symbolize the affection of surviving friends. As we consign to the grave the body of our deceased, we are reminded that there is also an immortal part within that shall survive the grave, and that shall never die.

Now we leave the future in the hands of God, the Creator, who is glorious in holiness, boundless in mercy, almighty in power, infinite in understanding, and who will do all things well.

Graveside Prayer:

Soul of the Universe, Creator of life, and Father of mankind: we commit back to nature only that which is natural, and to the grave only that which the grave can hold. To Thee, we commend the soul, trusting in Thy love, wisdom, and power. When the sense of sorrow and loneliness weighs heavily upon these, and the shadows deepen, faith falters and hope grows dim, draw us closer to Thee; encompass us in Thy love, sustain us by Thy Spirit, busy us in Thy service, chasten our desires with noble motives and keep ever vivid the memories of our dear one, until the night is passed and morn eternal dawns, through Jesus Christ our Lord. Amen.

Benediction:

Now may the Lord bless you and keep you, the Lord make His face to shine upon you, and be gracious unto you; the Lord lift up His countenance upon you, and give you peace. Amen.

Notes

Chapter I

1. J. B. Hernley, *Beyond Sorrow* (Cincinnati, Standard Publishing Company, 1938), p. 15.
2. *Ibid.*, Mrs. Southey.

Chapter II

1. Dorothy A. Thrupp.
2. Leslie R. Smith, *From Sunset to Dawn* (Nashville, Abingdon-Cokesbury Press, 1944), p. 48.
3. *Ibid.*, p. 41.
4. Henry Wadsworth Longfellow, "Gone to School."

Chapter III

1. Mrs. Joseph F. Knapp, "Open the Gates of the Temple" (New York, Carl Fischer, Inc.).
2. Charles L. Wallis, *The Funeral Encyclopedia* (New York, Harper & Brothers, 1953), prayer by Frank R. Snavely, p. 21.
3. *Ibid.*, p. 20, Francis Greenwood Peabody, "Of Such Is the Kingdom."
4. *Ibid.*, p. 59, from sermon by Harold E. Johnson.
5. *Ibid.*, p. 214, Robert Freeman, "Beyond the Horizon."
6. Edward Hopper.

Chapter IV

1. Geoffrey O'Hara and Daniel S. Twohig, "I Walked Today Where Jesus Walked" (New York, G. Schirmer, Inc., 1937).
2. E. L. Godkin in W. Halsey Smith, *A Service Book* (National Selected Morticians, 1953), p. 189.
3. Henry Wadsworth Longfellow, "Resignation."
4. John Henry Newman.

Chapter V

1. Andrew W. Blackwood, *The Funeral* (Philadelphia, Westminster Press, 1942), p. 117, quoted from *The Directory for Public Worship,* Presbyterian Church of England.
2. George Matheson.
3. James Whitcomb Riley, "Away," from *Afterwhiles* (Indianapolis, The Bobbs-Merrill Company, Inc.).
4. Philip James Bailey, "We Live in Deeds," from "Festus."
5. Charles L. Wallis, *op. cit.,* p. 259, "The Open Door," by Grace Coolidge.
6. *Ibid.,* p. 190, from sermon by William A. Tyson, Jr.
7. Francis G. Peabody, *Prayers for Various Occasions and Needs* (Boston, Houghton, Mifflin Co., 1930).
8. William Williams.

Chapter VI

1. "There Is No Death," copyright by Chappell and Company, Inc. Used by permission.
2. W. Halsey Smith, *op. cit.,* p. 150, "How Beautiful To Be with God," from *Wayside Altar.*
3. Charles L. Wallis, *op. cit.,* p. 196, "Let Them In, Peter," by Elma Dean, quoted in sermon by Howard J. Chidley.
4. From New York *Herald Tribune,* 1942, "I Die at Dawn," by Kees X—.

Chapter VII

1. William H. Bathurst.
2. Oliver Wendell Holmes, from "The Chambered Nautilus."
3. Edwin Markham, "An Epitaph," from *Poems of Edwin Markham,* Charles L. Wallis, ed. (New York, Harper & Brothers, 1950).
4. William Cullen Bryant, "Thanatopsis."

Chapter VIII

1. H. G. Spafford.
2. George Matheson, "O Love, That Wilt Not Let Me Go."
3. Charles L. Wallis, *op. cit.*, p. 255, from "The Victors," by Charles Hanson Towne.
4. From Introduction by Will Rogers to Charles Russell, *Trails Plowed Under* (New York, Doubleday & Co., Inc., 1927).

Chapter IX

1. James Montgomery.
2. Edgar Guest, "When Sorrow Comes," from *When Day Is Done* (Chicago, Reilly & Lee Company, 1929).
3. Henry Wadsworth Longfellow, "Resignation."
4. Dr. Dan Poling, *Faith Is Power* (New York, Greenberg Publisher, 1950), pp. 29, 30.
5. "Leave It There," C. Albert Tindley (Chicago, Hope Publishing Company).

Chapter X

1. Horatius Bonar, "I Heard the Voice of Jesus Say."
2. "But When Life Tumbles In, What Then?" from Arthur John Gossip, *The Hero in Thy Soul* (New York, Charles Scribner's Sons, 1929).
3. Charles L. Wallis, *op. cit.*, p. 25, Roselle Mercier Montgomery, "On the Death of an Aged Friend."

Chapter XI

1. John Greenleaf Whittier.

Chapter XII

1. Ray Palmer.
2. Charles Wesley.

Chapter XIII

1. G. Edwin Osborn, ed., *Christian Worship: A Service Book* (St. Louis, The Bethany Press, 1953), p. 93.
2. Author unknown.

Chapter XIV

1. Thomas Moore.
2. John Stainer.
3. John Greenleaf Whittier.
4. Adapted from St. Francis Assisi.

Chapter XV

1. George Matheson.
2. Temple Bailey, *A Little Parable for Mothers* (Westwood, N.J., Fleming H. Revell Company, 1936).

Chapter XVI

1. Isaac Watts.
2. Strickland Gillilan.
3. Rufus Jones, source unknown.
4. W. D. Cornell.

Chapter XVII

1. John Greenleaf Whittier.
2. John MacNeill, *Many Mansions* (New York, Doran, 1926), pp. 130, 131.
3. Grantland Rice.

Chapter XVIII

1. Fanny J. Crosby.
2. Henry van Dyke, from *Book of Common Worship* (Philadelphia, Westminster Press, 1905–06).
3. Charles L. Wallis, *op. cit.*, p. 255, from "The Victors," by Charles Hanson Towne.

Chapter XIX

1. Isaac Watts.
2. Frederick W. Faber.

Chapter XX

1. William Walsham How.
2. Henry F. Lyte.
3. Washington Gladden.

4. W. Halsey Smith, *op. cit.*, p. 188, quoted from Rev. Robert J. Burdette.
5. Alfred Tennyson, "Crossing the Bar."
6. John Henry Newman.

Chapter XXI

1. Frederick W. Faber.
2. Charles F. Wallis, *op. cit.*, Robert Freeman, "Beyond the Horizon."
3. Grantland Rice.
4. J. B. Hernley, *op. cit.*, p. 27, "The Weaver," anonymous.

Chapter XXII

1. Frederick W. Faber.

Chapter XXIII

1. Jane Crewdson.
2. Author unknown.
3. Bishop Berggrav quoted in *Christian Leader* (Elgin, Illinois, David C. Cook Publishing Co.), December 30, 1956.
4. G. Edwin Osborn, *op. cit.*, p. 111.